Latin Letters

Reading Roman Correspondence

FOCUS CLASSICAL COMMENTARIES

Latin Letters

Reading Roman Correspondence

Cecelia A. E. Luschnig

Illustrated by Dona Black

Focus An Imprint of
Hackett Publishing Company
Indianapolis/Cambridge

ISBN 10: 1-58510-198-2
ISBN 13: 978-1-58510-198-6

Previously published by Focus Publishing / R. Pullins Company
Focus An Imprint of
Hackett Publishing Company
www.hackettpublishing.com
P.O. Box 44937
Indianapolis, Indiana 46244-0937

Printed in the United States of America

18 17 16 15   6 7 8 9 10

CONTENTS

PREFACE

Reading almost anything in Latin, even the old standards of the nineteen-fifties high school curriculum, has been a great joy and adventure to me. At almost fifteen I was reading Caesar in second year Latin and upon learning about the "forced march," my best friend and I forced ourselves to walk from our school on 68th and Lexington home to Fort Washington Avenue and 184th. We made it, but never tried it again. The next year Cicero's overblown rhetoric was another treat and the beginning of a long history of writing "memo bombs" full of anaphora and other choice oratorical devices that added excitement and occasionally peril to an otherwise routine teaching and writing career. Such was the curriculum at every high school in New York. In senior year, at sixteen or seventeen, we were mature enough to read Vergil, the classic of western civilization.

It was later in life that I discovered lighter reading could be enjoyable and even rewarding, especially the pleasure of reading other people's mail, that meant for publication, of course. My first year at Idaho—where I have spent most of my career—for the first time I taught a full course in Pliny's letters and to my great satisfaction I found that the students actually enjoyed reading them and were able to make the transition from Wheelock's *sententiae* to connected Latin with relatively little pain. Letters are good for this level, when the students have learned their forms, syntax, and basic vocabulary but now are faced with putting everything together. The letters are short and self-contained. The subject matter is varied and timely. And sometimes the writing is as fine as anything in Latin prose.

The two hearts of the present collection are Cicero and Pliny, because these two epistolographers offer the most absorbing content and reveal the most engaging personalities. The texts are accompanied by notes and glosses to reduce the frustration of students in a first or second Latin reading course. Important vocabulary words are marked with an asterisk because students at this stage do not have the experience to know which words are common and which rare. A modest amount of vocabulary study, English derivatives, notes on word formation, and compounding rules, is included in the notes (and in Appendix II). Words that a student can easily figure out, whether from a close English derivative or by separating the word into its elements, are not glossed. I hope that this practice will give the students more confidence when faced with a page of Latin. Students who own the *Collins Gem Dictionary* (which is recommended as a convenient and inexpensive yet full and accurate dictionary) might consider using it to build their vocabulary by putting a mark beside any word they need to look up; if a check mark is already beside the word in question, the student will know that it is time to learn that word. Ideally, the *Oxford Latin Dictionary* will be available in the school or college library for lexical investigations, which offer students entry into the world of primary research.

Some grammar review is also encouraged. Suggestions for review are made in the notes to most of the longer letters of Cicero and Pliny. An appendix summarizes the points that I have found students most need to review in the third and fourth semesters: the uses of the cases; pronouns of nearly any kind; formation and use of the subjunctive; conditions; gerunds and gerundives. There is also a summary of deponent verbs used by Pliny. As reference grammar, I recommend Allen and Greenough's *New Latin Grammar* (A&G).

I would like to thank my Latin teachers, Mrs. Eileen Fitzgerald, Mr. Irving Kizner, Dr. Thelma DeGraff, Professors I. E. Drabkin, Miriam Drabkin, Robert Hennion, and Carl Trahman, and nearly forty years of Latin students, who among them taught me Latin, helped me learn how to teach it, and made it feel worthwhile and enjoyable. Thanks also to Lance Luschnig with whom years ago I spent a happy summer reading Cicero's letters and who encouraged me to undertake this project.

LIST OF ABBREVIATIONS

< derived from
> becomes or produces as a derivative
(1) indicates a first conjugation verb
A&G = Allen and Greenough, *New Latin
   Grammar*
abl. = ablative
abl. abs. = ablative absolute
acc. = accusative
a.d. = ante diem
ad Att. = *ad Atticum*
ad Fam. = *ad Familiares*
adj. = adjective
ad Q.F. = *ad Quintum Fratrem*
adv. = adverb
an. = anno (in the year)
Ann. = *Annales* of Tacitus
A.U.C. = ab urbe condita
b. = born
C. = Gaius
ca. = circa
Cn. = Gnaeus
compar. = comparative
conj. = conjunction
d. = died
d. = *dedi* or *data* (at end of a letter)
D. = Decimus
dat. = dative
depon. = deponent
dimin. = diminutive
Engl. = English
Ep. = *Epistulae*
f. = feminine
Febr. = Februarius
frag. = fragment
freq. = frequentative
fut. = future
gen. = genitive
Gk. = Greek
Gn. = Gnaeus

Hist. = *Historiae*
HS = sesterce (Roman monetary unit)
imperf. = imperfect (tense)
indecl. = indeclinable
inf. = infinitive
interj. = interjection
interrog. = interrogative
K. or Kal. = Kalendae
L. = Lucius
lit. = literally
loc. = locative
m. = masculine
m. = mense (in the month)
M. = Marcus
M. f. = Marci filius
m/f. = masculine or feminine
n. = neuter, noun
NH = *Natural History, Naturalis Historia*
nom. = nominative
Non. = Nonae (Nones)
OLD = *Oxford Latin Dictionary*
P. = Publius
pass. = passive
perf. = perfect (tense)
pl. = plural
prep. = preposition
Q. = Quintus
Quint. = Quintilis (July)
rel. = relative
S. or Sal. = salutem
S.D. = salutem dicit
S.P.D. = salutem plurimam dicit
Sp. = Spurius
sing. = singular
subj. = subjunctive
superl. = superlative
T. = Titus
v. = verb
voc. = vocative

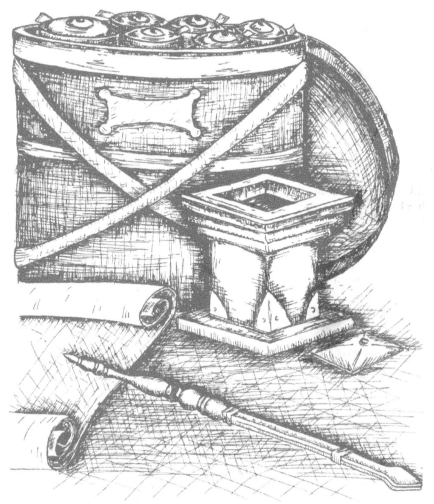

Ancient writing tools: stylus, papyrus sheet, ink pot, papyrus case.

INTRODUCTION

Epistulae sunt Romanae: **a literary genre of their own**

Satura nostra tota est (Quintilian: "Satire is ours alone"). The Romans keenly felt their debt to Greek cultural innovation and achievement in ambiguous and very human ways. Greek was the educated Roman's second language. For higher education young men of the upper classes went to Athens or Rhodes or other down-at-heels university towns in what were once the glorious lands of Greece. They admitted that they had borrowed or stolen the plastic and pictorial arts and the other genres of literature: epic, lyric, rhetoric, tragedy, comedy, philosophy, history from the Greeks, claiming only satire as their own invention or at least as the art they had perfected. On the other hand, a suspicion of things Greek was also a constant in Roman society. From time to time all philosophers (Greeks) would find themselves expelled from Rome. Old-fashioned Romans would inveigh against the decadence of Greek culture and on occasion even turn ignorance (a feigned ignorance in the case of Cato the Censor) of the Greek tongue into a virtue.

Not Satire, however, whose genealogical credentials are rather mixed, but letters, genuine correspondence, other people's mail, are the major contribution of Latin speakers to the development of the literary genres. What is so great about that? We can easily imagine an austere old Roman and equally a middle-aged administrator of public education asking such a question. In the face of cliché-ridden post cards and hastily written, ungrammatical, abbreviation-laden e-mail and text-messaging or despised daily blogs (correspondence or journalism?), it behooves a letter-lover to offer something in the way of an answer.

The Greeks, of course, wrote letters. *Epistulae* is, after all, a word derived from Greek (ἐπιστολή *something sent by messenger*). But what kinds of letters did they write and what letters have survived from the Hellenes? We have some private epistles in Greek, but not until rather late from literary persons. Among papyrus documents more or less randomly preserved in Egypt, a son writes home for money, another asks for forgiveness of past unfilial behavior, a husband tells his pregnant wife to raise their child only if it is a boy. There are extant business letters, diplomatic and official correspondence, and formal philosophical or didactic theses pretending to be letters (like Plato's letter on forms of government or Isocrates' epistle to Nicocles on how to be a good prince). I have to admit, however, to a certain degree of affection for the preserver of Epicurus' letters, since they represent the bulk of his surviving work, but they are not what we would call letters. In short these are documents of social, economic, political, or intellectual history, but not letters. In addition we have fictional letters attributed to the famous or infamous. Some are school exercises run amok; others are expressions from the imaginations of later writers creating memoirs, something like inchoate modern epistolary novels. What we do not have from the ancient Hellenes are collections of personal, private correspondence such as would give us a picture of a whole person, a personality captured among the immediate and specific concerns, activities, feelings of everyday life. In Latin letter-writing, for the first time, a full human personality enters western literature and, even more startling, is recoverable to us. In defining the "phenomenon of Cicero," Brooks Otis (in "The Uniqueness of Latin Literature," ARION VI.1 (1967):189) writes:

> The fact seems to be that Greeks did not care to write or preserve their letters as a concrete, unique moment in a specific personality and a specific milieu. This is why we can realize Cicero, can penetrate his personal history, his day-to-day experience, as we simply cannot realize or penetrate any of the Greeks. There is certainly more here than an accident: Romans valued and so preserved what Greeks, certainly the classical Greeks, did not value or preserve to anything like the same degree.

History is not just the big picture. Private lives inside houses, little pleasures, anxieties over petty things, personal hopes, pride, disappointments give meaning to the sweep of events and make them universal.

Personalities on papyrus or in wax: the Roman letter writers

Collections of personal correspondence began to come into circulation in the first century B.C.E. with the publication of Cicero's letters after his death. In the next few generations, although we have a few letters of Augustus preserved in the imperial archives and even a fragment of a letter written by Vergil, the main body of extant Roman letters hardly qualifies as personal: the philosophical epistles of Seneca, which would fit more comfortably in the Greek type of formal essays masquerading as letters. It is not until the second century C.E. and the epistolary collection of the younger Pliny that we return to genuine personal correspondence, and even these are rather more carefully written than Cicero's, keeping usually to a single topic and to formal rules of composition. Other collections follow, those of Fronto to Marcus Aurelius, and later of Ausonius, Symmachus, and Sidonius Apollinaris, and of the well-known Christian writers. A selection of letters of Cicero and Pliny forms the heart of this introductory collection.

To many readers, Cicero is the finest writer of the Latin language in prose. His orations and, to a lesser extent, his philosophical essays have been read by generations of Latin students, beginning already in his own lifetime. We know more about the politics of his age than any other period in antiquity, in large part because of contemporary events in which he himself took part and about which he wrote, and from the works of other writers both contemporary and later. But these writings do not give us a picture of a human life. For a more complete Cicero, we have 37 books of personal letters in four separate collections to friends, family, colleagues: *ad Atticum* (16 books), *ad Familiares* (16), *ad Brutum* (2), *ad Quintum fratrem* (3). Most of these are his own, but about a hundred (from *ad Fam.*) were written by various other people in answer to Cicero and were preserved in the collection made by his freedman, secretary, and friend, Tiro, who had made and saved copies. More than any other classical writings these are informal, freely written, idiomatic. They jump from topic to topic often with amazing unconcern for the rules of composition. Many of them appear to be unedited and in the case of the letters to Atticus (Cicero's best friend) and those to his brother Quintus, were originally written in his own hand and not through a scribe.

The letters of Pliny the Younger give us a second and almost equal, though considerably smaller, body of personal writing. But Pliny's are more carefully written and arranged: he himself uses the words *curatius* (I.1), *curiosius* (IX.28.5), *diligentius* (VII.9.8) of his own and others' letters. It is clear that by his time books of *Epistulae* already formed a recognized literary undertaking. In *Ep.* VII.9.8, for example, Pliny recommends letter-writing as a way to develop *pressus sermo purusque*, "a style that is at once restrained/dense and unadorned/clear" (see also IX.2.1-4 where he compares his own letters to Cicero's). Each of the letters is usually confined to a single theme and is in itself complete (as indeed are some of Cicero's, such as the letter to his relative Marius about the games held in Rome on the occasion of the dedication of Pompey's theater, *ad Fam.* VII.1). Most of Pliny's letters avoid the excessive length of essays and, if longer than usual, include an apology for the length. His style in the letters is polished, poetic, rhetorical.

Pliny's letters were published in ten books, of which the first nine are his personal correspondence and the tenth his correspondence with the Emperor Trajan before and during his time as Imperial legate to Bithynia with special powers to fix the financial administration of the province, a position for which he seems to have been very well suited. The letters are not arranged in chronological order, though in general the different books consist of letters from the same year or two. They are not entirely random either. Pliny clearly spent some effort on arrangement, to give each book a variety of subject matter and of persons addressed. Book Nine is the most diffuse and is thought by some scholars to have been something of a rush job as Pliny was clearing up loose ends before setting off on his imperial mission.

Typical subjects of his letters are: life in the city, literature and the writing of it, country life and leisure, recommendations, portraits of illustrious men and women, descriptions and narratives, trials and politics.

Although Pliny's letters, unlike Cicero's, were gathered, rewritten and arranged with a view to publication, they still can be seen as the genuine communication of a cultured Roman to his circle of other cultured Romans. They reveal his concerns, interests, affections, aspirations, and anxieties. Cicero too had in mind to edit his letters (*ad Att.* XVI.5.6), but seems not to have had the opportunity. He discusses the classification of letters in *ad Fam.* II.4 to Curio:

> *Epistularum genera multa esse non ignoras sed unum illud certissimum,*
> *cuius causa inventa res ipsa est, ut certiores faceremus absentis si quid esset*
> *quod eos scire aut nostra aut ipsorum interesset. Huius generis litteras a me*
> *profecto non exspectas. Tuarum enim rerum domesticos habes et scriptores*
> *et nuntios, in meis autem rebus nihil est sane novi. Reliqua sunt epistularum*
> *genera duo, quae me magno opere delectant, unum familiare et iocosum,*
> *alterum severum et grave.*

"You are not unaware that there are many kinds of letters, but this
one is most obvious, which is the raison d'être for the genre itself, that is,
to inform those who are absent if there is any news they should know or
we want them to know. A letter of this type you certainly do not expect
from me. For of your own affairs you have in your own household both
writers and messengers. And of mine there is nothing new to tell. There
are two other kinds of letter in which I take considerable pleasure, the
one the friendly and whimsical, the other the serious and austere."

Survival of the Quotidian: physical properties of the Roman letters

A typical Roman letter was written on papyrus (*charta*) with a pen (*calamus*)
and ink (*atramentum*). Multiple pages (if needed) were glued together and the
whole was rolled and sealed and given to a carrier (*tabellarius*) or friend who was
traveling to the vicinity of the recipient to deliver in person or to pass on through
another intermediary. It is hard to imagine anyone setting out on a journey
without a satchel, at least, of epistles to friends and friends of friends along the
way. There were, furthermore, slaves, one of whose duties was to visit the harbor
at docking times in the hope of letters (see *ad Fam.* XVI.5). Not until imperial
times did the Romans have anything like a postal service. Hastier notes, especially
those requiring a swift answer, were written on slim wooden tablets (*codicilli*) that
were covered with wax and inscribed with a stylus (see *ad Q.F.* II.10). The original
could then be smoothed over and the rescript written and returned immediately.
A famous example of such an urgent note is found in Pliny VI.16: *Egrediebatur*
domo: accipit codicillos Rectinae Tasci inminenti periculo exterritae, "[Pliny the
Elder] was about to leave the house when he is handed a tablet from Rectina the
wife of Tascius alarmed by the threatening peril [of Vesuvius]." Instead of replying,
he set out immediately in person.

Cicero's letters to Atticus and those to his brother were saved by their
recipients. Tiro, Cicero's secretary, made copies of the letters that form the books
in *ad Familiares* and glued them together into rolls which then formed the volumes
(*volumen*, "something rolled"). In a letter to Atticus (XVI.5), Cicero writes that
although "there is no collection of my letters, Tiro has about seventy and there
are also some to be obtained from you. I should look through these and make
emendations. Only then will they be published" (*mearum epistularum nulla*
est συναγωγή; *sed habet Tiro instar septuaginta, et quidem sunt a te quaedam*

sumendae. eas ego oportet perspiciam, corrigam; tum denique edentur). Cicero never found the time or opportunity to edit his correspondence. It is not known who edited and published the letters, nor when they were published, but it is not unlikely that Tiro—who, despite his long and serious illnesses (see *ad Fam.* xvi.5), outlived his former master by about four decades—was responsible for the publication of *ad Familiares* during the Augustan period. The form in which they have survived is according to recipients, with all of Book Fourteen being addressed to Cicero's wife Terentia and their children and Book Sixteen being to or about Tiro. Other addressees include just about all the well-known actors on the political stage, literary and scholarly figures, old friends, and young proteges. The letters to Atticus were probably published later, but had been made available to Cicero's friends after his death. The arrangement is roughly chronological. Unfortunately Atticus' replies were not ever published and there are many gaps in our understanding of the meaning of many specifics in Cicero's letters to him.

Pliny, writing about 150 years later, opens the first of his books of epistles with a short message of dedication to Septicius Clarus in which he explains in what is probably a literary fiction that he has undertaken the publication at his friend's urging and has collected examples of rather carefully (*paulo curatius*) composed letters. The epistolary collection of the fifth century bishop Sidonius Apollinaris also opens with such a dedication and explanation to his friend Constantius, a fellow priest, in which he compares his more polished (*politiores*) letters to those of Symmachus and Pliny.

From the start both these men see their letters as literary compositions to end in publication. The authenticity of Pliny's letters as correspondence has been questioned, but many factors urge us to believe in their genuineness, not least their precise minor details, whether of business and household affairs or of personal matters in the letters of advice, recommendation, and consolation. Pliny took great pleasure in writing, a fact that is most obvious in his letters of description of natural phenomena and in the (sometimes contrived) playfulness of his style. It is generally agreed (see Sherwin-White 20-65) that the first nine books of Pliny's epistles were published sometimes singly and sometimes in groups of two or three books between 104 and 109 c.e., but several in Book One refer to earlier events and it is reasonable to think that they were written close to the time described. Book Ten (of his letters to Trajan and the emperor's rescripts) was published after Pliny's death possibly by Suetonius, the well-known archivist and biographer, who accompanied him to Bythinia.

Letters from emperors, whatever their style or content, demand our interest. Augustus' letters, however, reveal an affectionate grandfather and uncle who calls his heir a young donkey and finds his heart going out to the awkward Claudius, his grandnephew. The fiscal conservative Trajan shows an affection for the solicitous Pliny, and seems truly concerned to be seen as, and to be, a decent person and a good governor. The other letters in this collection are of interest mostly as social documents: a birthday invitation from an officer's wife posted in Vindolanda along Hadrian's Wall; the pleading letter of Cornelia to her son Gaius Gracchus trying to prevent him from getting himself killed as his brother had done; the letter from Vergil to Augustus telling him that the *Aeneid* needs more work. Finally two later letters, one from Ausonius, often called "the first of the Christian poets" and another from Sidonius Apollinaris, bishop of Auvergne, give us a peek at the genre as it continued to the verge of the Middle Ages.

In our world of the personal in which—whether in novels, movies, reality television, even journalism—the individual counts for everything, where would we be without Tiro's heroic labor of love in preserving and passing on the letters of his sometime master, employer, friend, and admirer?

Letter-writing formulas

Faced with a blank page, we always know how to start a letter to a friend: "Dear ___". Closing can be more problematical. Do we write, "Yours sincerely" or "Love" or something in between? The ubiquity of e-mail has relaxed the rules, with its bantering informality tempered by smiling faces in various expressions. There are distinct formulas for opening and closing a Roman letter.

Salutation:

The name of the sender in the nominative and the name of the recipient in the dative followed by a word or words of greeting usually abbreviated:

CICERO ATTICO SAL.

SAL. = *salutem* (literally, "health") which stands for *salutem dicit*, "says hello" or "sends greetings".

M. CICERO S. D. M. MARIO

S. D. = *salutem dicit*

Sometimes with the name in the dative *suo* or *suae* is added to show affection:

TULLIUS S. D. TERENTIAE SUAE

SENECA LUCILIO SUO SALUTEM

C. PLINIUS SEPTICIO SUO S.

In this collection, in those letters where the salutation has survived only Augustus ignores this convention, beginning the letter to his grandson AVE, MI GAI.

To close a letter, a writer may either use no closing (as Cicero often does) or simply end with *Vale* or *Valete* (if there are two or more recipients, as in Cicero's letters to his wife and children), from *valeo, -ere* "be well", as a greeting, "farewell". There is no need for the writer to add his/her name, as we do, because it is already at the top of the letter. Except for his letters to the emperor Trajan, Pliny's letters all end with *Vale*.

Investigations

Sample Topics for Research and Writing

1. General
   — Collect idioms and useful expressions in the letters: this makes a good group project with individual students each taking a letter or a certain number of lines. The collections are then gathered and distributed to the class.
   — Collect additions for the grammar appendices: this helps make the grammar review a more active and participatory exercise. Again the additions can be distributed to the class.
   — Choose one letter and make a full commentary on it. Include in it:
      a polished translation
      the historical context
      persons, places, and things mentioned in the letter
      idioms and useful expressions
      unusual or difficult grammar
      style (for advanced students)
      text (for advanced students): are there variants or difficulties in the text? [For this a scholarly edition must be consulted.]
   — A comparison of two or more of the letter writers
   — The physical nature of letters
2. Individual writers or individual letters
   Cicero
      Cicero's campaign for office
      Cicero and Clodius
      Cicero and Atticus
      Cicero's family life
      Cicero and Terentia
      Cicero's estates
      Public games
      Pompey and Cicero
      Cicero's reading of Lucretius
      Cicero and Quintus
      Tiro, Cicero's freedman and editor
      Embassy to Antonius in Jan. 43 (*ad Fam.* XII.4)
      Posting letters
   Seneca
      Seneca's style
      Seneca's use of vocabulary
      Seneca's use of quotations

Pliny
    The arrangement of Pliny's letters
    Roman villas and their parts, indoors and out
    Como in Pliny's time and other Comans to whom he writes
    The career of Pliny the Elder
    The writings of Pliny the Elder
    Pliny and the eruption of Vesuvius
    Daily life in the city [ceremonies, business]
    Pliny's villas
    Treason trials and professional *delatores* (informers)
    Women in Pliny's letters
    The family of Arria and Fannia
    Schooling in Rome and the provinces
    Subjects taught in school
    Funding of education
    Length of time spent in school
    Tacitus' reputation as master of eloquence
    Pliny and his family
    Pliny and Calpurnia
    Pliny's light verse
    Pliny in Bithynia
    Water supplies and other public works
    The imperial post
Various other people's mail
    Cornelia's style/politics
    Vergil's modesty
    Augustus' use of Greek
    Trajan's letters: his own or the imperial secretariat's?
    The Vindolanda letters: subjects, materials, discovery
    Ausonius and Sidonius: who were these people and why do we
       not know more about them?

PART ONE

SELECTIONS FROM CICERO'S LETTERS

Marcus Tullius Cicero's life and career (as the leading orator of his day, consul at a time of crisis, participant in all the events of his day at the end of the Roman Republic, influential writer on philosophy and rhetoric) are well known from the quantity and quality of his surviving work. His letters, written between 68 and 43 B.C.E., from the death of his cousin Lucius to the year of his own death, chronicle the birth of his son, his campaign for office, the ups and downs of his marriage, sundry business and literary affairs, his tastes in art and entertainment, the illness of his beloved freedman and his precious daughter's death, and especially the crises of his political and personal life, including details from the most trivial to the most momentous. They reveal a man of wit, loyalty, affection, and courage as well as a man full of anxiety, indecision, inconstancy, and many other contradictions; in short, a person like ourselves.

Important Dates in Cicero's Life (all dates B.C.E.)

106 b. in Arpinum, 3 January.

89   Military service in the Marsic War under Gn. Pompeius Strabo.

79-8 Travel in Greece and Asia.

77   Return to Rome; marriage to Terentia.

75-74 Quaestor in Sicily.

69   Curule aedile.

68   First extant letter (*ad Att.* I.5).

66   Praetor.

65   Birth of Marcus, M.f., beginning of campaign for the consulate (*ad Att.* I.2).

64   Elected consul.

63   Consul, Catilinarian conspiracy.

61   Return of Pompey to Rome (*ad Att.* I.13).

58   Driven into exile by Clodius (*ad Att.* III.3, *ad Fam.* 14.2).

57   Recalled from exile.

55   Second consulate of Pompey and Crassus (*ad Fam.* VII.1, *ad Q.F.* 2.10, *ad Att.* IV.10).

54   Murder of Clodius.

51   Cicero proconsul in Cilicia.

50   Leaves Cilicia (*ad Fam.* XVI.5).

49   Civil War. Cicero joins Pompey in Greece (*ad Fam.* XIV.14, XIV.21).

48   Battle of Pharsalus; murder of Pompey. Cicero returns to Italy (*ad Fam.* XIV.8).

47   Caesar pardons Cicero (*ad Fam.* XIV.15, XIV.23).

46   Cicero divorces Terentia (cf. *ad Fam.* XIV.20).

45   Death of Tullia.

44   Assassination of Caesar (*ad Fam.* XII.4).

43   Death of Cicero, 9 December.

Letter 1: *Epistulae ad Atticum* I.2
Birth of Marcus, Catiline's trial, etc.

Scr. Romae m. Quint. an. 689 (65 B.C.E.).

CICERO ATTICO SAL.

(1) L. Iulio Caesare, C. Marcio Figulo consulibus filiolo me auctum scito salva Terentia. abs te tam diu nihil litterarum! ego de meis ad te rationibus scripsi antea diligenter. hoc tempore Catilinam competitorem nostrum defendere cogitamus. iudices habemus quos voluimus, summa accusatoris voluntate. spero, si absolutus erit, coniunctiorem illum nobis fore in ratione petitionis; sin aliter acciderit, humaniter feremus.

Scr. Romae m. Quint. an. 689: **scr.** = **scriptum** or **scripta** [**epistula**]. **Romae** (loc.). **m.** = **mense. Quint.** = **Quintili** < **Quintilis** July. **an.** = **anno.**

Cicero Attico Sal. This is the formula for addressing a letter. See introduction, page 6.

Atticus was Cicero's closest friend and his publisher.

Review: ablative absolute (appendix A: abl. B 11; A&G 419-420); future conditions (A&G 516); gerundives (A&G 503-7); indirect statement (A&G 577-80).

·1   **L. Iulio Caesare, C. Marcio Figulo consulibus:** the usual way of dating a year (by the names of the two consuls) is here humorously adapted by Cicero to mean the day of the election of Caesar and Figulus, taken by him to be an auspicious day for the birth of his son, Marcus, and at the same time informing Atticus of the election results. **scito** fut. imperative, *know!*, colloquial for "I am pleased to inform you." **salva Terentia**: abl. absolute; cf. our "mother and baby are doing fine." **ego de meis ad te rationibus**: the unusual ordering of the words is accounted for by Cicero's tendency to put pronouns as close together as possible. **Catilina**: the infamous Catiline who was threatened with prosecution on his return from his stint in Africa where he had recouped his failing fortune at the expense of the governed. Cicero did not, in fact, join in Catiline's defense. **competitor, -oris, m.** *fellow candidate* for office; a campaign for office is called *petitio* or *competitio*. **summa accusatoris voluntate**: abl. absolute of attendant circumstances. **accusator, -oris, m.** *prosecutor*; the prosecutor was Clodius (later Cicero's bitter enemy) who was in collusion with Catiline. The prosecutor had the right of *reiectio* (like our peremptory challenge) of any jurors who might be disposed to convict. **coniunctiorem**: sometimes candidates for office joined forces to defeat the other rivals. ***fore** = **futurum esse. aliter** (adv.) *otherwise.* **humaniter** (adv.) *like a human being* (Mensch), *with equanimity, philosophically.*

(2) tuo adventu nobis opus est maturo; nam prorsus summa
hominum est opinio tuos familiaris nobilis homines adversarios
honori nostro fore. ad eorum voluntatem mihi conciliandam
maximo te mihi usui fore video. qua re Ianuario mense, ut
constituisti, cura ut Romae sis.

2   **tuo adventu**: abl. with **opus est**. *opus est *there is need for* (+ abl.). **prorsus**
(adv.) *absolutely*. **nobilis homines**: those who had among their ancestors one
or more consuls. They opposed Cicero because he was a *novus homo*, a citizen
without any senatorial ancestors. On courting the *nobiles*, see Quintus Cicero's
Commentariolum Petitionis (*Campaign Handbook*) 1 and 4. For the past thirty
years only nobles had been elected to the consulate. *honos, -oris, m. *public
office*; **nostri honori** *my election* (to the consulate). **maximo usui**: dat. of
purpose. **constituo**, -ere, -stitui *resolve, arrange*. Atticus has lived in Greece
for twenty years and now is needed back to help with Cicero's campaign. He
seems to have returned home and stayed for three years: the next letter to him
is dated to 61 B.C.E. On a similar political topic see *ad Att.* I.1 in which Cicero
writes about where his campaign stands in July of 65. Of Catiline's candidacy–
should he be acquitted– he writes: *Catilina, si iudicatum erit meridie non
lucere, certus erit competitor.*

Letter 2: Ad Atticum I.5
Various family matters and business dealings

Scr. Romae initio anni 687 (67 B.C.E.).

CICERO ATTICO SAL.

(1) Quantum dolorem acceperim et quanto fructu sim privatus et forensi et domestico Luci fratris nostri morte in primis pro nostra consuetudine tu existimare potes. nam mihi omnia quae iucunda ex humanitate alterius et moribus homini accidere possunt ex illo accidebant. qua re non dubito quin tibi quoque id molestum sit, cum et meo dolore moveare et ipse omni virtute officioque ornatissimum tuique et sua sponte et meo sermone amantem adfinem amicumque amiseris.

(2) quod ad me scribis de sorore tua, testis erit tibi ipsa quantae mihi curae fuerit ut Quinti fratris animus in eam esset is qui esse deberet. quem cum esse offensiorem arbitrarer, eas litteras ad eum misi quibus et placarem ut fratrem et monerem ut minorem et obiurgarem ut errantem. itaque ex iis quae postea saepe ab eo ad me scripta sunt confido ita esse omnia ut et oporteat et velimus.

This is the earliest surviving letter of Cicero. Notice how he changes the subject in every sentence of this newsy missive, perhaps because he is responding to Atticus' letters or just jumping around as he thinks of items of interest to add.

Review indirect question (A&G 573-6).

1   *fructus, -us, m. *enjoyment, profit.* **Lucius** was Cicero's cousin and had helped him gather evidence against Verres for a case he prosecuted. **pro nostra consuetudine** *in view of our close friendship, considering our aquaintance.* **nostra** = Cicero's and Atticus'. **humanitate et moribus**: hendiadys: *culture and ways = cultured ways, kindly words.* **ornatissimus**, -a, -um *richly endowed.* **tui**: objective genitive with **amantem**, the participle. **adfinis**, -is *relation by marriage*: Lucius' cousin, Cicero's younger brother Quintus was married to Atticus' sister, Pomponia.

2   *quod *as to the fact that.* **quantae curae**: predicate genitive. **ut**: introducing a noun clause after **curae**. **offensior** (compar. adj.) *rather annoyed, causing offense.* **eas litteras ... quibus**: introduces a relative clause of characteristic or purpose. **placo** (1) *appease.* **obiurgo** (1) *reproach.*

(3) de litterarum missione sine causa abs te accusor. numquam enim a Pomponia nostra certior sum factus esse cui dare litteras possem, porro autem neque mihi accidit ut haberem qui in Epirum proficisceretur nequedum te Athenis esse audiebamus.

(4) de Acutiliano autem negotio quod mihi mandaras, ut primum a tuo digressu Romam veni, confeceram; sed accidit ut et contentione nihil opus esset et ut ego, qui in te satis consili statuerim esse, mallem Peducaeum tibi consilium per litteras quam me dare. etenim cum multos dies auris meas Acutilio dedissem, cuius sermonis genus tibi notum esse arbitror, non mihi grave duxi scribere ad te de illius querimoniis, cum eas audire, quod erat subodiosum, leve putassem. sed abs te ipso qui me accusas unas mihi scito litteras redditas esse, cum et oti ad scribendum plus et facultatem dandi maiorem habueris.

(5) quod scribis, etiam si cuius animus in te esset offensior, a me recolligi oportere, quid dicas neque id neglexi, sed est miro quodam modo adfectus. ego autem quae dicenda fuerunt de te non praeterii; quid autem contendendum esset ex tua putabam voluntate me statuere oportere. quam si ad me perscripseris, intelleges me neque diligentiorem esse voluisse quam tu esses neque neglegentiorem fore quam tu velis.

---

3   **de litterarum missione** *concerning the sending of letters.* **nequedum** *and not yet.* **audiebamus** a past epistolary tense: though the writer is speaking of a present circumstance, he/she projects it into the future when the recipient will read it, by which time it will be in the past.

4   **Acutilianus** *of Acutilius*; this was an ongoing and tedious business deal (see *ad Att.* 1.4 and I.8). **a tuo digressu** *after parting from you.* **confeceram**: epistolary pluperfect: "I meant to finish it." **contentio, -onis, f.** *hurry, haste, effort.* **Peducaeum**: subject of **dare**; Sextus Peducaeus, a friend of both Cicero and Atticus. **duxi** I *thought.* **subodiosum** *a tad of a nuisance, something of a bore*; the prefix *sub-* diminishes the burden. **leve puto** *make light of.* **reddo, -ere, redidi, redditum** *deliver.*

5   **cuius** refers to L. Lucceius, with whom Atticus has a tiff. **recolligo** *bring together, get hold of, build up someone's affections.* **contendo, -ere** *make an effort, assert, allege, maintain.*

(6) de Tadiana re mecum Tadius locutus est te ita scripsisse, nihil esse iam quod laboraretur, quoniam hereditas usu capta esset. id mirabamur te ignorare, de tutela legitima, in qua dicitur esse puella, nihil usu capi posse.

(7) Epiroticam emptionem gaudeo tibi placere. quae tibi mandavi et quae tu intelleges convenire nostro Tusculano velim, ut scribis, cures, quod sine molestia tua facere poteris. nam nos ex omnibus molestiis et laboribus uno illo in loco conquiescemus.

(8) Quintum fratrem cotidie exspectamus. Terentia magnos articulorum dolores habet. et te et sororem tuam et matrem maxime diligit salutemque tibi plurimam ascribit et Tulliola deliciae nostrae. cura ut valeas et nos ames et tibi persuadeas te a me fraterne amari.

---

6   **Tadiana re**: a case of disputed property. **laboro** (1) *trouble.* **hereditas usu capta** *right of possession.* **usus, -us,** m. *the use by legal right of property owned by another, usufruct* (the right to use another's property and receive the profits). **mirabamur**: epistolary imperfect. It is impossible to tell whether he means "I" or "we" including others who are involved in the case. **tutela legitima**: *legally prescribed guardianship.* Tadius has no right to the property while the heir to it was still a ward and Cicero is surprised that Atticus does not know this.

7   **Epiroticam emptionem** refers to the estate purchased at Buthrotum in Epirus. **convenio, -ire** *be suitable.* **Tusculanum**: Cicero's recently acquired estate near Tusculum. **velim cures**: *please take care of.*

8   **Terentia**: Cicero's wife. **Tulliola** dimin. of Tullia, Cicero's daughter of whom he is very fond (see **deliciae meae**).

Letter 3: Ad Atticum I.13
Letters received, order of speaking in the Senate; Clodius affair, etc.

Scr. Romae vi K. Febr. an. 695 (61 B.C.E.).

CICERO ATTICO SAL.

(1) Accepi tuas tris iam epistulas, unam a M. Cornelio quam
Tribus Tabernis, ut opinor, ei dedisti, alteram quam mihi
Canusinus tuus hospes reddidit, tertiam quam, ut scribis, ancora
soluta de phaselo dedisti; quae fuerunt omnes, ut rhetorum
pueri loquuntur, cum humanitatis sparsae sale tum insignes
amoris notis. quibus epistulis sum equidem abs te lacessitus
ad rescribendum; sed idcirco sum tardior quod non invenio
fidelem tabellarium. quotus enim quisque est qui epistulam paulo
graviorem ferre possit nisi eam perlectione relevarit? accedit
eo quod mihi non ut quisque in Epirum proficiscitur, ita ad te
proficisci videtur. ego enim te arbitror caesis apud Amaltheam
tuam victimis statim esse ad Sicyonem oppugnandum profectum
neque tamen id ipsum certum habeo quando ad Antonium
proficiscare aut quid in Epiro temporis ponas. ita neque Achaicis
hominibus neque Epiroticis paulo liberiores litteras committere
audeo.

Review: future passive periphrastic (A&G 158 d); subjunctive with verbs of fearing
   (A&G 564).

vi K. Febr. *January 27.*

1   **a M. Cornelio**: M. Cornelius delivered the letter entrusted to him by Atticus.
Tribus Tabernis: Tres Tabernae a little over 30 miles from Rome along the
Appian Way on the way to Brundisium, from which Atticus set sail for Greece.
Canusinus *at Canusinum*, a town on the way to Brundisium. **ancora soluta**
(usually **sublata**): *the anchor weighed* (lit. *released*). The expression is usually
ancora sublata or **ora soluta**; the text as it stands is either a copyist's error,
or Atticus telescopes the two expressions. **phaselus**, -i, m. *a light ship*, the
boat that took Atticus to his ship and by which he sent the last of the three
letters. **rhetorum pueri** (from the Greek phrase ῥητόρων παῖδες) *the
professional orators.* **sparsae** < **spargo**, -ere, -si, -sum *strew, sprinkle.* ***insignis,**
-e *distinguished, marked.* **lacesso**, -ere, -ivi, -itum *challenge, provoke.* **idcirco**
(adv.) *for this* (the following) *reason.* ***tabellarius**, -i, m. *letter carrier, messenger.*
quotus quisque *in what proportion to the total number is each one who?* i.e. *there
are not many who.* **perlectio**, -onis, f. *a read-through, perusal.* **relevo** (1) *lighten.*
***accedit eo** *there is added to that, in addition.* ***quod** *the fact that.* ***proficiscor,**

(2) Sunt autem post discessum a me tuum res dignae litteris nostris, sed non committendae eius modi periculo ut aut interire aut aperiri aut intercipi possint. primum igitur scito primum me non esse rogatum sententiam praepositumque esse nobis pacificatorem Allobrogum, idque admurmurante senatu neque me invito esse factum. sum enim et ab observando homine perverso liber et ad dignitatem in re publica retinendam contra illius voluntatem solutus, et ille secundus in dicendo locus habet auctoritatem paene principis et voluntatem non nimis devinctam beneficio consulis. Tertius est Catulus, quartus, si etiam hoc quaeris, Hortensius. consul autem ipse parvo animo et pravo tamen cavillator genere illo moroso quod etiam sine dicacitate ridetur, facie magis quam facetiis ridiculus, nihil agens cum re publica, seiunctus ab optimatibus, a quo nihil speres boni rei publicae quia non vult, nihil speres mali quia non audet. eius autem conlega et in me perhonorificus et partium studiosus ac defensor bonarum.

-i, profectus/a sum *set out, march forth*. **caesis victumeis** (archaic spelling of victimis): Cicero uses the language of military campaigning for Atticus' setting out for Sicyon to see about debts owed him. **Amalthea**, the nymph, symbolizing plenty, to whom Atticus had a shrine on his estate and to whom he is pictured sacrificing before his campaign. **Sicyon**, a city in Macedonia which was in Atticus' debt. **oppugno** (1) *beseige*. **Antonius**: governor of Macedonia; he had been Cicero's colleague in the consulate. **Achaicus**, -a, -um *of the province of Achaia*. **liberiores** *rather frank, more confidential.*

2   **intereo**, -ire, -ivi/ii, -itum *die, be lost*. **primum me** ... this refers to the privilege of speaking first in the Senate, granted to a former consul. In this case it was given to C. Calpurnius Piso who had been governor of Gallia Narbonensis where the principal tribe, the Allobroges, were in revolt. **pacatorem** (< pax, pacis > paco, -are) is sarcastic. **admurmuro** (1) *grumble at/against*. **observo** (1) *take notice, pay attention to*. **perversus**, -a, -um *wrong-headed, ill-natured*. **contra illius voluntatem** *in spite of him*. **solutus**, -a, -um *released from*. **principis** [loci]. **Q. Lutatius Catulus** leader of the *Optimates*. **Q. Hortensius**, a leading orator, rival of Cicero. **consul**: the consul is M. Pupius Piso Frugi, a person of varied talents who had been close to Cicero earlier. **parvo animo et pravo**: abl. of description; notice the play on words. **cavillator** -oris, m. *jester, jeerer*. **dicacitas** -tatis, f. *mordant mockery, caustic ridicule*. **facie** ... **facetiis**: abl. of cause. **seiungo**, -ere, -iunxi, -iunctum *separate, dissociate*. **optimates**: *the aristocratic party*. **collega**: his *colleague* in office was M. Valerius Messalla Niger. **perhonorificus**, -a, -um *very respectful*. **partium**: gen. *political party* (gen. with **studiosus**). **studiosus**, -a, -um *actively engaged in; learned in* (+ gen.).

(3) qui nunc leviter inter se dissident. sed vereor ne hoc quod infectum est serpat longius. credo enim te audisse, cum apud Caesarem pro populo fieret, venisse eo muliebri vestitu virum, idque sacrificium cum virgines instaurassent, mentionem a Q. Cornificio in senatu factam (is fuit princeps, ne tu forte aliquem nostrum putes); postea rem ex senatus consulto ad virgines atque ad pontifices relatam idque ab iis nefas esse decretum; deinde ex senatus consulto consules rogationem promulgasse; uxori Caesarem nuntium remisisse. in hac causa Piso amicitia P. Clodi ductus operam dat ut ea rogatio quam ipse fert et fert ex senatus consulto et de religione antiquetur. Messalla vehementer adhuc agit severe. boni viri precibus Clodi removentur a causa, operae comparantur, nosmet ipsi, qui Lycurgei a principio fuissemus, cotidie demitigamur, instat et urget Cato. quid multa? vereor ne haec neglecta a bonis, defensa ab improbis magnorum rei publicae malorum causa sit.

(4) Tuus autem ille amicus (scin quem dicam?), de quo tu ad me scripsisti, postea quam non auderet reprehendere, laudare coepisse nos, ut ostendit, admodum diligit, amplectitur, amat, aperte laudat, occulte sed ita ut perspicuum sit invidet. nihil come, nihil simplex, nihil ἐν τοῖς πολιτικοῖς inlustre, nihil honestum, nihil forte, nihil liberum. sed haec ad te scribam alias subtilius; nam neque adhuc mihi satis nota sunt et huic terrae filio nescio cui committere epistulam tantis de rebus non audeo.

---

3   **qui** refers to the two consuls. **dissideo, -ere** *disagree*. **infectus, -a, -um** (< **inficio**) *spoiled, corrupt*. **cum pro populo**: "when at the offering of sacrifice." **instauro** (1) *celebrate anew*. **Q. Cornuficius**: a pretorian, i.e. not one of us (**nostrum**), the consulars. **princeps** *the first* (i.e. to speak against Clodius). **virgines** *Vestals*. **rogationem promulgo** *give notice of a bill*. **nuntium remisisse** *sent notice* (of divorce): this was Caesar's second wife, Pompeia. **antiquo** (1) *to reject a bill, to vote not to adopt a bill*. **operae comparantur** *rowdies* or *thugs are being hired*. **Lycurgei**: *Lycurgans*, after the 4th c. orator who was a zealous prosecutor. **demitigo** (1) *make mild*.

4   **tuus amicus** = Pompey: Cicero often avoids naming names in politically sensitive matters. **comis, -e** *courteous*. ἐν τοῖς πολιτικοῖς *in politics*. **subtilius** (compar. adv.) *with more precision, more exactly*. **terrae filius** *son of the earth*. ***nescioquis**, nescioquid *I know not who, some obscure* (person). Latin is rich in indefinite pronouns (see Appendix B).

(5) Provincias praetores nondum sortiti sunt. res eodem est loci quo reliquisti. Τοποθεσίαν quam postulas Miseni et Puteolorum includam orationi meae. "A. d. iii Non. Decembr." mendose fuisse animadverteram. quae laudas ex orationibus, mihi crede, valde mihi placebant sed non audebam antea dicere; nunc vero quod a te probata sunt, multo mi ἀττικώτερα videntur. in illam orationem Metellinam addidi quaedam. Liber tibi mittetur, quoniam te amor nostri φιλορήτορα reddidit.

(6) Novi tibi quidnam scribam? quid? etiam. Messalla consul Autronianam domum emit HS cxxxiiii. "quid id ad me?" inquies. tantum quod ea emptione et nos bene emisse iudicati sumus et homines intellegere coeperunt licere amicorum facultatibus in emendo ad dignitatem aliquam pervenire. Teucris illa lentum negotium est sed tamen est in spe. tu ista confice. A nobis liberiorem epistulam exspecta. vi Kal. Febr. M. Messalla, M. Pisone coss.

5   *sortior, -iri, -itus/a sum *draw lots* (for assigned duties or provinces). τοποθεσίαν [topothesian] *description of a place*. **A. d. iii Non. Decembr.** = ante diem iii Nonas Decembris, that is *3 December*. **mendose** (adv.) *full of faults, faulty, mistaken* (with **fuisse**). **quae = ea quae.** ἀττικώτερα [attikotera] *more Attic, more in the Attic* [Athenian] *style*, a pun on Atticus' name which he earned from his association with Athens. **Metellinus, -a, -um** *against Metellus Nepos*. **nostri = mei:** objective gen. with **amor.** φιλορήτορα [philorhetora] *lover of oratory*.

6   *etiam *yes*. **HS cxxxiiii** = *13,400,000 sesterces*: this was a lot, but not unheard of; Cicero paid 3,500,000 for his house on the Palatine (see. *ad Fam*. V.6.2). Numbers are notoriously unreliable due to miscopying. **Autronianam domum** *the town house of P. Autronius Paetus* (who was in exile because of his participation in the Catilinarian conspiracy). **"quid id ad me?"** idiom, *what does it have to do with me?* **inquies** < fut. of *inquam, inquis, inquit*. **facultas, -tatis,** f. *means, resources*. **pervenio, -ire** *to have recourse to*. **Teucris** is an unknown woman who acted as an intermediary in securing a loan for Cicero from C. Antonius; this Greek name may be code for Antonius' wife or other woman who should not be openly named. **negotium, -i,** n. a colloquialism like χρῆμα in Greek; *business, of a* person in derogatory sense.

Letter 4: *Epistulae ad Familiares* VII.1
The Games in Rome

Scr. Romae A.U.C. 699 (58 B.C.E.).

M. Cicero S. D. M. Mario

(1) Si te dolor aliqui corporis aut infirmitas valetudinis tuae
tenuit, quo minus ad ludos venires, fortunae magis tribuo quam
sapientiae tuae; sin haec, quae ceteri mirantur, contemnenda
duxisti et, cum per valetudinem posses, venire tamen noluisti,
utrumque laetor, et sine dolore corporis te fuisse et animo
valuisse, cum ea, quae sine causa mirantur alii, neglexeris,
modo ut tibi constiterit fructus otii tui, quo quidem tibi perfrui
mirifice licuit, cum esses in ista amoenitate paene solus relictus.
Neque tamen dubito, quin tu in illo cubiculo tuo, ex quo tibi
Stabianum perforasti et patefecisti Misenum, per eos dies
matutina tempora lectiunculis consumpseris, cum illi interea,
qui te istic reliquerunt, spectarent communes mimos semisomni.
Reliquas vero partes diei tu consumebas iis delectationibus, quas
tibi ipse ad arbitrium tuum compararas, nobis autem erant ea
perpetienda, quae Sp. Maecius probavisset.

M. Mario: Marcus Marius, possibly a Marian relative of Cicero from Arpinum;
he lived in retirement near Cicero's villa at Pompeii. Melmoth in his Everyman
edition writes: "the person to whom this letter is addressed, seems to have been of
a temper and constitution, that placed him far below the ambition of being known
to posterity." This letter, unlike most Ciceronian epistles keeps close to a single
theme and is more like an essay, in the manner of Pliny's letters.

Review subjunctive with verbs of hindering (A&G 558); cum with subjunctive
(A&G 546, 549).

1   **aliqui**, -qua, -quod adj. *some or other*. **dolor** ... Marius suffered from gout
(podagra: *ad Fam.* VII.4). *****quo minus** (+ subjunctive) *so as to prevent
something from happening, so that not*. **ludos**: the magnificent *games* produced
by Pompey for the dedication of the theatre (see Pliny the Elder *NH* VIII.7).
fortunae, sapientiae: dat. with **tribuo**. **per valetudinem** *as far as your health
was concerned*. *****uterque**, utraque, utrumque *each of the two*; **utrumque**:
internal acc. with **laetor** (1, depon. *be glad*) *on either account*. **modo ut** (+
subjunctive) *provided only that*. **consto**, -are, constiti *be, exist*. **fructus**, -us, m.
profit. **quo**: abl. with **perfrui**. **in ista amoenitate**: cf. Pliny *Ep.* IV.16: *erat enim
frequens amoenitas orae* where he is talking about the same coast at the time

(2) Omnino, si quaeris, ludi apparatissimi, sed non tui stomachi;
coniecturam enim facio de meo; nam primum honoris causa in
scenam redierant ii, quos ego honoris causa de scena decessisse
arbitrabar; deliciae vero tuae, noster Aesopus, eiusmodi fuit, ut
ei desinere per omnes homines liceret: is iurare cum coepisset,
vox eum defecit in illo loco: "si sciens fallo." Quid tibi ego alia
narrem? nosti enim reliquos ludos, qui ne id quidem leporis
habuerunt, quod solent mediocres ludi; apparatus enim spectatio
tollebat omnem hilaritatem, quo quidem apparatu non dubito
quin animo aequissimo carueris; quid enim delectationis habent
sexcenti muli in *Clytaemnestra* aut in *Equo Troiano* creterrarum
tria milia aut armatura varia peditatus et equitatus in aliqua
pugna? quae popularem admirationem habuerunt, delectationem
tibi nullam attulissent.

---

of its destruction. **Stabianum sinum** *the Stabian side of the bay*. **perforando**
[**pariete**] *by cutting through the wall*. **matutinus, -a, -um** *morning* (cf. Engl.
Matins, matutinal). **lectiunculus, -i,** m. *short, light reading*. **communes:**
possibly in contrast to the solitude Marius is enjoying, *in common*; or if
communis with **mimos** *common*. **mimus, -i,** m. *pantomime* who performed
in farces. **ad arbitrium tuum** *to your taste/liking*. **comparo** (1) *get ready for
a course of action, provide*. **perpetior, -i** (compound of *patior*) *undergo, suffer
through*. **Sp.** (Spurius) **Maecius Tarpa** was appointed by Pompey to choose
the plays to be performed at the games.

2   **tui stomachi:** gen. of characteristic *to your taste*. **honoris causa** (1) as a
compliment to Pompey (2) for the sake of their reputations. **deliciae tuae**
your favorite. **noster Aesopus:** Clodius Aesopus, a friend of Cicero, a leading
tragic actor known for the beauty of his voice, probably a freedman (from his
Greek name). **desino, -ere, -ivi/ii** *retire*. **iuro** (1) *swear, take an oath*; although
some scholars have taken this to mean that actors take an oath not to deceive
before performing, it seems to defeat the purpose of being an actor. Others,
more reasonably, take this and the words "**si sciens fallo**" to refer to a line of
the (now lost) play the actor was performing. **lepos, -oris,** m. *charm, grace*.
apparatus, -s, m. *display*. **careo, -ere, -ui** *lack, miss, do without*. **sescenti, -ae,
-a** *six hundred*. **mulus, -i,** m. *mule*. **Clytemnestra,** a tragedy by Accius. *Equo
Troiano, Trojan Horse*, a tragedy by Livius Andronicus or Naevius. **creterra**
(an archaic form, probably a word used in the play) *mixing bowl* (part of the
spoils of war displayed in the tragedy). **armatura, -ae,** f. *armor, equipment*.
peditatus, -us, m. *infantry, foot-soldiers*. **equitatus, -us,** m. *cavalry*.

(3) Quod si tu per eos dies operam dedisti Protogeni tuo, dummodo is tibi quidvis potius quam orationes meas legerit, ne tu haud paulo plus quam quisquam nostrum delectationis habuisti; non enim te puto Graecos aut Oscos ludos desiderasse, praesertim cum Oscos vel in senatu vestro spectare possis, Graecos ita non ames, ut ne ad villam quidem tuam via Graeca ire soleas. Nam quid ego te athletas putem desiderare, qui gladiatores contempseris? in quibus ipse Pompeius confitetur se et operam et oleum perdidisse. Reliquae sunt venationes binae per dies quinque, magnificae—nemo negat—, sed quae potest homini esse polito delectatio, cum aut homo imbecillus a valentissima bestia laniatur aut praeclara bestia venabulo transverberatur? quae tamen, si videnda sunt, saepe vidisti, neque nos, qui haec spectavimus, quidquam novi vidimus. Extremus elephantorum dies fuit: in quo admiratio magna vulgi atque turbae, delectatio nulla exstitit; quin etiam misericordia quaedam consecuta est atque opinio eiusmodi, esse quandam illi beluae cum genere humano societatem.

---

3   *quodsi *but if.* **Protogenes**, -is a slave whose job was to read to Marius. *dummodo (+ subjunctive) *provided that.* *ne (adv.) *truly;* used before a pronoun. **haud paulo plus** *not a little more = a lot more.* **delectionis**: partitive gen. with **plus**. **nostrum**: partitive gen. with **quisquam**. **Oscos ludos**: *Atellan farces.* **vel** *even.* **in senatu vestro** *in the local city council.* **via Graeca** probably an old inland road, alternate route to the newer coastal road. **oleum** *oil.* **et operam et oleum perdere** proverb: *to waste effort and oil (expense)* This is a pun: oil was used for lamps (as in "to burn the midnight oil") and athletes rubbed themselves with oil. **venatio**, -onis, f. *wild beast hunts;* competitions between men and beasts. **bini**, -ae, a *two each.* **politus**, -a, -um *polished, accomplished, refined.* **imbecillus**, -a, um *weak.* **lanio** (1) *tear, maul.* **venabulum**, -i, n. *hunting spear.* **transverbero** (1) *strike through, pierce through.* **misericordia**, -ae, f. *pity, compassion.* **societas**, -tatis, f. *companionship, fellowship.* Pliny *NH* 8.1 identifies the elephant as the greatest of the animals and closest to humanity: *Maximum est elephans proximumque humanis sensibus.* See Pliny the Elder, *NH* 8.21-2 on the reaction of the crowd to the pitiful plight of the elephants.

(4) His ego tamen diebus, ne forte videar tibi non modo beatus, sed liber omnino fuisse, dirupi me paene in iudicio Galli Caninii, familiaris tui. Quod si tam facilem populum haberem, quam Aesopus habuit, libenter mehercule [artem] desinerem tecumque et cum similibus nostri viverem; nam me cum antea taedebat, cum et aetas et ambitio me hortabatur et licebat denique, quem nolebam, non defendere, tum vero hoc tempore vita nulla est; neque enim fructum ullum laboris exspecto et cogor nonnumquam homines non optime de me meritos rogatu eorum, qui bene meriti sunt, defendere.

(5) Itaque quaero causas omnes aliquando vivendi arbitratu meo teque et istam rationem otii tui et laudo vehementer et probo, quodque nos minus intervisis, hoc fero animo aequiore, quod, si Romae esses, tamen neque nos lepore tuo neque te—si qui est in me—meo frui liceret propter molestissimas occupationes meas; quibus si me relaxaro—nam, ut plane exsolvam, non postulo—, te ipsum, qui multos annos nihil aliud commentaris, docebo profecto, quid sit humaniter vivere. Tu modo istam imbecillitatem valetudinis tuae sustenta et tuere, ut facis, ut nostras villas obire et mecum simul lecticula concursare possis.

(6) Haec ad te pluribus verbis scripsi, quam soleo, non otii abundantia, sed amoris erga te, quod me quadam epistula subinvitaras, si memoria tenes, ut ad te aliquid eiusmodi scriberem, quo minus te praetermisisse ludos poeniteret: quod si assecutus sum, gaudeo; sin minus, hoc me tamen consolor, quod posthac ad ludos venies nosque vises neque in epistulis relinques meis spem aliquam delectationis tuae.

---

4   *forte (adv.) *perchance.* disrumpo/dirumpo, -ere, -rupi, -ruptum *burst, break apart.* L. Caninius Gallus: an active supporter of Pompey. *iudicium, -i, n. *trial.* taedet, -ere, -uit (impersonal) *weary, cause weariness.* vita nulla est *there is no life, life is not worth living.* *non numquam *sometimes.*

5   *aliquando (adv.) *ever, some day.* abitratu meo *at my own discretion.* interviso, -ere *look after, visit at times.* postulo (1) *demand, ask.* commento (1) *think about, occupy one's mind with.* lecticula, -ae, f. *litter.*

6   erga (+ acc.) *towards.* subinvito (1) *suggest, sort of invite.* quo minus = ut eo minus. *sin minus *if not.*

Letter 5: *Ad Quintum Fratem* II. 10
Lucretius etc.

Scr. mense Februario A.U.C. 700 (54 B.C.E.).

MARCUS QUINTO FRATRI SALUTEM.

(1) Epistulam hanc convicio efflagitarunt codicilli tui; nam res quidem ipsa et is dies, quo tu es profectus, nihil mihi ad scribendum argumenti sane dabat; sed, quemadmodum, coram cum sumus, sermo nobis deesse non solet, sic epistulae nostrae debent interdum alucinari.

(2) Tenediorum igitur libertas securi Tenedia praecisa est, cum eos praeter me et Bibulum et Calidium et Favonium nemo defenderet; de te a Magnetibus ab Sipylo mentio est honorifica facta, cum te unum dicerent postulationi L. Sestii Pansae restitisse. Reliquis diebus si quid erit, quod te scire opus sit, aut etiam si nihil erit, tamen scribam quotidie aliquid: pridie Idus neque tibi neque Pomponio deero.

Review relative clauses of characteristic (A&G 534-5).

1   **convicium**, -i, n. *outcry, clamor, wrangling.* **efflagito** (1) *demand urgently, insist,* i.e. *demand a reply.* **codicilli**: *tablets* made of thin pieces of wood and covered with wax. They were used for short notes and were particularly handy when an immediate reply was desired. **argumentum**, -i, n. *argument, proof.* **argumenti**: partitive gen. with **nihil**. **coram** (adv.) *face to face; in person.* *interdum (adv.) *sometimes, from time to time.* **alucinor** (1) *wander in mind, ramble* [> Engl. *hallucinate*].

2   **Tenediorum libertas**: refers to a petition to grant the island of Tenedos the status of a free community which was rejected with profound unconcern. **securi Tenedia**: *with the axe of Tenedos,* a proverbial expression meaning swift and decisive action, after king Tenes' axe which was used to behead all adulterers, including his own son. **securis**, -s, f. *axe* (< **seco** *cut*). **Bibulus,** Calpurnius Bibulus, consul with Caesar in 59. **Calidius,** an orator of praetorian rank. **Favonius,** a companion and supporter of Cato. **Magnetibus ab Sipylo** *Magnesians near Sipylus* (i.e. in Lydia, to distinguish them from the other Magnesians in Caria). **Magnetes** *the inhabitants of Magnesia.* **resto,** -are, -stiti *resist* + dat. **postulatio**, -onis, f. *demand.* The **Pansa** referred to here is unknown; it has been speculated that he was a tax-farmer (or publican). **pridie Idus** *the day before the Ides,* i.e. the 12th. **Pomponius** = Atticus.

(3) Lucretii poemata, ut scribis, ita sunt: multis luminibus ingenii, multae etiam artis; sed, cum veneris, virum te putabo, si Sallustii *Empedoclea* legeris, hominem non putabo.

Letters 6-11: *Ad Familiares*
Book XIV. 2; 14; 21; 8; 15; 23
Family dramas

The letters in Book 14 of Cicero's *ad Familiares* are addressed to his wife Terentia. These letters display Cicero's great affection for his family and they attest to the strength, courage, loyalty, and independence of his wife Terentia in caring for their family in Rome and protecting their assets over the long periods of Cicero's absence: his eighteen months of exile; his stint as proconsul of Cilicia, and his time serving Pompey in the Civil War. Later letters are less clear in showing affection and determination to stay in the marriage. She wrote often, sometimes every day, as is apparent from the fact that many of his are replies to hers. Unfortunately Terentia's letters have not survived.

The earliest letter in the series (XIV.4) was written at the beginning of Cicero's exile, to Terentia and their children at Rome. When Cicero fled from Rome after his consulship, in fear of prosecution for the questionable legality of his handling of the Catilinarian conspiracy, his enemies persuaded the Senate to banish him for illegally executing Roman citizens who had been co-conspirators. As a result, Cicero became a public enemy: his family was treated shabbily, his money was seized, and his house on the Palatine was looted and destroyed.

XIV.2 By the time of this letter Cicero had made his way to Thessalonica in Thessaly, where he remained from May to November of 58. Meanwhile, back at home, Terentia has been suffering indignities to both her person and property, for which Cicero blames himself. On August 4, 57 he was finally recalled from exile, returned to Italy, and was received by joyous throngs of welcoming citizens when he reached Rome on September 4. His property was restored and damages paid to him.

---

3   **Lucreti**: a rare reference in antiquity to the work of Lucretius, *De rerum natura*, recently published. **Sallustii** *Empedoclea*: Sallustius' *Empedocles*, perhaps a translation of the 5th c. B.C.E. Greek philosopher-poet Empedocles. **virum ... hominem** Cicero makes a witty contrast between a man or hero and a mere human with all the foibles that implies.

Scr. Thessalonicae a. d. III. Non. Oct. A.U.C. *696. (October 5, 58* B.C.E.*)*

TULLIUS S. D. TERENTIAE ET TULLIOLAE ET CICERONI SUIS

(1) Noli putare me ad quemquam longiores epistulas scribere, nisi si quis ad me plura scripsit, cui puto rescribi oportere; nec enim habeo, quod scribam, nec hoc tempore quidquam difficilius facio. Ad te vero et ad nostram Tulliolam non queo sine plurimis lacrimis scribere; vos enim video esse miserrimas, quas ego beatissimas semper esse volui idque praestare debui et, nisi tam timidi fuissemus, praestitissem.

(2) Pisonem nostrum merito eius amo plurimum: eum, ut potui, per litteras cohortatus sum gratiasque egi, ut debui. In novis tribunis pl. intellego spem te habere: id erit firmum, si Pompeii voluntas erit; sed Crassum tamen metuo. A te quidem omnia fieri fortissime et amantissime video, nec miror, sed maereo casum eiusmodi, ut tantis tuis miseriis meae miseriae subleventur: nam ad me P. Valerius, homo officiosus, scripsit, id quod ego maximo cum fletu legi, quem ad modum a Vestae ad tabulam Valeriam ducta esses. Hem, mea lux, meum desiderium, unde omnes opem petere solebant! te nunc, mea Terentia, sic vexari, sic iacere in lacrimis et sordibus, idque fieri mea culpa, qui ceteros servavi, ut nos periremus!

Review jussive noun clauses (A&G 563), result clauses (A&G 536-8), indirect question (A&G 573-5).

Terentia, Cicero's wife. **Tulliola** an affectionate diminutive of **Tullia**, Cicero's daughter. **Cicero**, his son Marcus. Cicero himself is called **Tullius**.

1 *noli *do not.* Instead of using **ne** with the imperative, Latin prefers to say "noli" pl. "nolite" "do not wish to" with the infinitive. Other ways of expressing prohibition are **ne** with the perfect subjunctive and **cave** with the present subjunctive. **queo** *be able.* **praesto** (1) *surpass, exhibit, show.*

2 **Pisonem**, Cicero's son-in-law, C. Calpurnius Piso Frugi. He died before Cicero's return from exile. **pl.** = plebis. **casus** -us, m. *fall, event, emergency.* **euismodi** *of such a kind* acts as an adjective with **casum** to lead to the result clause. **sublevo** (1) *lift from beneath, lighten, alleviate.*

(3) Quod de domo scribis, hoc est de area, ego vero tum denique mihi videbor restitutus, si illa nobis erit restituta; verum haec non sunt in nostra manu: illud doleo, quae impensa facienda est, in eius partem te miseram et despoliatam venire. Quod si conficitur negotium, omnia consequemur; sin eadem nos fortuna premet, etiamne reliquias tuas misera proiicies? Obsecro te, mea vita, quod ad sumptum attinet, sine alios, qui possunt, si modo volunt, sustinere, et valetudinem istam infirmam, si me amas, noli vexare; nam mihi ante oculos dies noctesque versaris: omnes labores te excipere video; timeo, ut sustineas. Sed video in te esse omnia; quare, ut id, quod speras et quod agis, consequamur, servi valetudini.

(4) Ego, ad quos scribam, nescio, nisi ad eos, qui ad me scribunt, aut [ad eos,] de quibus ad me vos aliquid scribitis. Longius, quoniam ita vobis placet, non discedam; sed velim quam saepissime litteras mittatis, praesertim si quid est firmius, quod speremus. Valete, mea desideria, valete, D. a. d. III. Non. Oct. Thessalonica.

officiosus, -a, -um *obliging, dutiful.* quem ad modum *how.* a [aede] Vestae: understand *temple.* ad tabulam Valeriam: often understood as referring to a *bank*, but more likely the offices of the Tribunes. Tabula can mean tablet, a counting board, auction notice, plaque, or painting; thus it may refer to a commemorative picture set up in or near the tribunal to which Terentia was dragged. Cicero suggests that those seeking his aid would ask his wife to intercede. vexari, iacere infinitives of exclamation with subjects in the accusative. vexo (1) *harass, afflict, upset.*

3   *area, -ae, f. *ground, building-site, lot*; Cicero's house on the Palatine had been burned to the ground so only the lot remained. restituo, -ere *restore, put back in its original position.* impensa [pecunia] *expense, cost, outlay.* By negotium he means the *business* of his return from exile. consequor, -i, secutus/a sum *follow, reach, attain.* *reliquiae -arum, f. pl. *remains, what is left.* proicio, -ere, -ieci, -iectum *throw out, let go, throw away.* sine imperative of *sino *permit.* verso (1) *keep turning, agitate.* servi imperative of servio.

4   D. = dedi or data.

XIV.14 Cicero had left Rome during Caesar's rapid advance on the city. He is worried about his wife and daughter who were staying behind.

Scr. Minturnis VIII Kalendas Februarias A.U.C. *705 (49* B.C.E.*)*

TULLIUS TERENTIAE ET PATER TULLIAE, DUABUS ANIMIS SUIS,
ET CICERO MATRI OPTIMAE, SUAVISSIMAE SORORI S. P. D.

(1) Si vos valetis, nos valemus. Vestrum iam consilium est, non solum meum, quid sit vobis faciendum. Si ille Romam modeste venturus est, recte in praesentia domi esse potestis; sin homo amens diripiendam urbem daturus est, vereor ut Dolabella ipse satis nobis prodesse possit. Etiam illud metuo, ne iam intercludamur, ut, cum velitis exire, non liceat. Reliquum est, quod ipsae optime considerabitis, vestri similes feminae sintne Romae; si enim non sunt, videndum est, ut honeste vos esse possitis. Quomodo quidem nunc se res habet, modo ut haec nobis loca tenere liceat, bellissime vel mecum vel in nostris praediis esse poteritis. Etiam illud verendum est, ne brevi tempore fames in urbe sit.

(2) His de rebus velim cum Pomponio, cum Camillo, cum quibus vobis videbitur, consideretis, ad summam animo forti sitis: Labienus rem meliorem fecit; adiuvat etiam Piso, quod ab urbe discedit et sceleris condemnat generum suum. Vos, meae carissimae animae, quam saepissime ad me scribite, et vos quid agatis et quid istic agatur. Quintus pater et filius et Rufus vobis s. d. Valete. VIII Kal. Minturnis.

Cicero = Cicero's son Marcus. **S. P. D.** = salutem plurimam dicunt.

Review future passive periphrastic and future active periphrastic (A&G 158, 195, 196).

1   **ille** = Caesar. **in praesentia esse** *be present.* ***sin** *but if.* **amens**, -entis *out of one's mind, amok.* ***ut** with verb of fearing *that not.* Cornelius **Dolabella**, Cicero's son-in-law, a partisan of Caesar. **intercludo**. -ere *cut off, block off.* **vestri**: gen. of pronoun **vos** with *similes*. **se res habet** + adv. (idiom) *the case stands.* **praedium**, -i, n. *estate.*

2   **Pomponius** =Atticus. **Camillus** was a legal expert whom Cicero consulted. **ad summam** *above all, to complete it all.* **Labienus** was a legate of Caesar who opposed him in the civil war. **Piso**: L. Calpurnius Piso, Caesar's father-in-law. **sceleris**: gen. of the penalty with **condemnat**. **quod** *in that.* ***gener**, -i, m. *son-in-law*, that is, Caesar. **Quintus pater et filius**: Cicero's brother and nephew. **Minturnis** [written] *at Minturnae.*

XIV.21, et seqq. Cicero had joined Pompey's forces in Greece, but had not joined in the battle of Pharsalus. He returned to Italy and remained in Brundisium for a year until Caesar forgave him and invited him back to Rome in 47 B.C.E. His letters to Terentia become less and less affectionate as these short examples show.

21 Scr. Brindisi 706 (48 B.C.E.)

Tullius Terentiae Suae S. D.

S. v. b. e. e. v. Da operam, ut convalescas; quod opus erit, ut res tempusque postulat, provideas atque administres et ad me de omnibus rebus quam saepissime litteras mittas. Vale.

8 Scr. in castris Pompeii a. d. IV. Non. Iun. a.u.c. 707 (June 2, 47 B.C.E.)

Tullius Terentiae Suae Sal.

Si vales, bene est, ego valeo. Valetudinem tuam velim cures diligentissime; nam mihi et scriptum et nuntiatum est te in febrim subito incidisse. Quod celeriter me fecisti de Caesaris litteris certiorem, fecisti mihi gratum. Item posthac, si quid opus erit, si quid acciderit novi, facies, ut sciam. Cura, ut valeas. Vale. D. IIII Non. Iun.

---

21   **S. v. b. e. e. v. Si vales, bene est, ego valeo.* Cicero often uses this formula in letters to his wife written in the years 48-7, but rarely in letters to his friends. **dare operam pay attention, do one's best.* *opus est *it is necessary.* *postulo (1) *demand.*

8   **febris, -is,** f. *fever.* **certum/certiorem facere** *assure, inform.* *facere gratum + dat. *do a favor, oblige.* *item adv. *likewise.* **facies ut** + subjunctive: *please be sure that.* *Cura, ut valeas: a formulaic closing like our "take care," or "be well." The letters of 48 and 47 B.C.E. often begin and end with such formulaic expressions (see XIV.8; XIV.21, 22, and 23), but the earlier letters, those from his exile, do not.

15 Scr. Brundisii XII. Kal. Quintil. a.u.c. 707 (June 19, 47 B.C.E.)

TULLIUS S. D. TERENTIAE

Si vales, bene est. Constitueramus, ut ad te antea scripseram, obviam Ciceronem Caesari mittere, sed mutavimus consilium, quia de illius adventu nihil audiebamus. De ceteris rebus, etsi nihil erat novi, tamen, quid velimus et quid hoc tempore putemus opus esse, ex Sicca poteris cognoscere. Tulliam adhuc mecum teneo. Valetudinem tuam cura diligenter. Vale. XII K. Quintiles.

23 Scr. Brundisii prid. Idus Sextiles a.u.c. 707 (August 12, 47 B.C.E.)

TULLIUS TERENTIAE SUAE S. D.

S. v. b. e. e. v. Redditae mihi tandem sunt a Caesare litterae satis liberales, et ipse opinione celerius venturus esse dicitur; cui utrum obviam procedam, an hic eum exspectem, cum constituero, faciam te certiorem. Tabellarios mihi velim quam primum remittas. Valetudinem tuam cura diligenter. Vale. D. pr.Id. Sext.

---

15 *constituo, -ere, -ui, -itum *decide.* antea *adv. *earlier, before.* *obviam *adv. used with verbs to imply motion [go] *to meet* [+ dat.]. **Ciceronem** is *M. Tullius Cicero M.f.,* the son of Cicero. **Sicca:** a friend of Cicero who owned a property at Vibo, a town in the toe of Italy.

23 *liberalis, -e *gracious, courteous.* **opinione** abl. of comparison with **celerius,** "more quickly than one might have supposed." *tabellarius, -i, m. *letter carrier;* since there was no postal service until Augustus' time, the delivery of letters depended upon *tabellarii,* private couriers. Some were maintained by the *publicani* with whom private individuals could arrange for the delivery of private letters; well-off people also had their own *tabellarii.*

Letter 12 *Epistulae ad Familiares* XVI. 5
Tiro's health

Scr. Leucade VII. Idus Novembres a.u.c. 704 (50 B.C.E.).

TULLIUS ET CICERO ET Q. Q.
TIRONI HUMANISSIMO ET OPTIMO SAL. PLUR. DIC.

(1) Vide, quanta sit in te suavitas: duas horas Thyrrei fuimus;
Xenomenes hospes tam te diligit, quam si vixerit tecum; is
omnia pollicitus est, quae tibi essent opus; facturum puto.
Mihi placebat, si firmior esses, ut te Leucadem deportaret, ubi
te plane confirmares: videbis, quid Curio, quid Lysoni, quid
medico placeat. Volebam ad te Marionem remittere, quem, quum
meliuscule tibi esset, ad me mitteres; sed cogitavi unas litteras
Marionem afferre posse, me autem crebras exspectare.

(2) Poteris igitur et facies, si me diligis, ut quotidie sit Acastus
in portu: multi erunt, quibus recte litteras dare possis, qui
ad me libenter perferant; equidem Patras euntem neminem
praetermittam. Ego omnem spem tui diligenter curandi in Curio
habeo: nihil potest illo fieri humanius, nihil **nostri** amantius:
ei te totum trade. Malo te paullo post valentem quam statim
imbecillum videre: cura igitur nihil aliud nisi ut valeas; cetera ego
curabo. Etiam atque etiam vale. Leucade proficiscens, VII. Id. Nov.

Book XVI consists of twenty-seven letters to or about Cicero's freedman, friend,
and secretary, Tiro. Cicero and his party are returning to Rome from his province,
Cilicia. Tiro had been ill for some time with stomach trouble and had to be left
behind at Patrae (Patras). Cicero writes from Leucas.

Review substantive result clauses (A&G 568).

Tullius: Marcus Tullius Cicero. **Cicero:** his son Marcus. **Q. Q.** his brother Quintus
and his brother's son Quintus. **SAL. PLUR. DIC.** *salutem plurimam dicunt.*

1   **Thyrrei** *at Thyrreum* in the north of Acarnania on the road from Actium to
     Athens. He is here referring to a stop on the outward journey. **Xenamenes** had
     possibly met Tiro at that time. **te confirmare** *get yourself stronger.* **Curius,** a
     friend of Atticus in business at Patrae, admired for his wit and urbanity. **Lyso,**
     -onis, Cicero's host at Patrae. **medico:** a doctor named Asclapo (mentioned in
     an earlier letter). **Mario,** -onis, a slave of Cicero. **meliuscule** (adv.) *somewhat
     better, a little better.*

2   **poteris** [facere]. *****quotidie** (adv.) *daily, every day* [> Engl. *quotidian*]. **Acastus**
     one of Cicero's slaves who had the task of meeting ships in the hope of receiving
     letters. **etiam atque etiam** *again and again, once again.*

Letter 13: *Ad Familiares* xii.4
The Ides of March and after

Scr. Romae mense Februario A.U.C. *711 (43* B.C.E.*)*

CICERO CASSIO SAL.

(1) Vellem Idibus Martiis me ad coenam invitasses: reliquiarum nihil fuisset. Nunc me reliquiae vestrae exercent, et quidem praeter ceteros me: quamquam egregios consules habemus, sed turpissimos consulares, senatum fortem, sed infimo quemque honore fortissimum. Populo vero nihil fortius, nihil melius Italiaque universa. Nihil autem foedius Philippo et Pisone legatis, nihil flagitiosius; qui quum essent missi, ut Antonio ex senatus sententia certas res denuntiarent, quum ille earum rerum nulli paruisset, ultro ab illo ad nos intolerabilia postulata rettulerunt: itaque ad nos concurritur, factique iam in re salutari populares sumus.

C. **Cassius** Longinus, one of the conspirators against Caesar. "Yon Cassius has a lean and hungry look."

Review independent uses of the subjunctive (A&G 439-47)

1   **coena** = cena *dinner, banquet.* ***reliquiae**, -arum, f. pl. *leftovers, leavings;* he means especially Marcus Antonius (Marc Antony). **exerceo** -ere *engage in, exercise, harass, persecute.* **quamquam ... habemus:** "true we have." **infimo quemque honore fortissimum** *the lower their rank the more bold/ brave/ firm;* **quisque** with the superlative. **infimus** *lowest.* **fortissimum** [**est**]. Those in the lowest rank are the **Quaestorii**. Marcus **Philippus** was one of the ambassadors (**legati**) sent by the Senate to Antony in January 43. L. Calpurnius **Piso** Caesoninus another of the ambassadors to Antony. ***legatus**, -i, m. *ambassador.* This refers to the embassy sent to Antony at Mutina demanding that he leave Cisalpine Gaul or risk war. The third member of the delegation, Servius Sulpicius, died before reaching Antony's camp. The others, Philippus and Piso, returned to Rome on February 1 with Antony's counterdemands and the Senate proclaimed a state of war. The next day Cicero delivered his eighth Phillipic (denouncing Antony). **flagitiosus**, -a, -um *disgraceful.* ***quum** = cum. **ex senatus sententia** *in accordance with a resolution of the Senate.* **certas res** *specific items,* i.e. not to lay siege to Mutina, not to attack the consul elect, not to loot the province of Gaul, not to levy recruits, to lead his army to this side of the Rubicon and come no closer than 200 miles from the city, and to submit to the Senate and People of Rome (see *Philippics* VI.4 and VII.26). **paruisset** < **pareo**, -ere, -ui (+ dat.) *submit to, comply with.* ***ultro** (adv.) *of one's own accord, unasked, actually.* That is, "they took it upon themselves" (Shackleton Bailey). ***popularis**, -e *belonging to the people;* that is, *a darling of the people, a popular favorite.*

(2) Sed, tu quid ageres, quid acturus, ubi denique esses, nesciebam: fama nuntiabat te esse in Syria; auctor erat nemo. De Bruto, quo propius est, eo firmiora videntur esse, quae nuntiantur. Dolabella valde vituperabatur ab hominibus non insulsis, quod tibi tam cito succederet, quum tu vixdum xxx dies in Syria fuisses; itaque constabat eum recipi in Syriam non oportere. Summa laus et tua et Bruti est, quod exercitum praeter spem existimamini comparasse. Scriberem plura, si rem causamque nossem: nunc, quae scribo, scribo ex opinione hominum atque fama. Tuas litteras avide exspecto. Vale.

2   M. Iunius **Brutus**, the tyrannicide (of *et tu, Brute* fame). Cassius and Brutus were in Athens in the fall of 44. Brutus had then advanced into Macedonia and Cassius had gone to Syria.

Dolabella, Cicero's ex-son-in-law; the province of Syria had been assigned to him in April. The joke (implied by the word *insulsis*) is that although thirty days was the period allowed for a governor to remain in his province after the arrival of his successor, Cassius is not even to be allowed thirty days from the beginning of his governorship. It fact, however, Cassius had no legal right to Syria, but the clause **itaque ... oportere** implies that Cassius should hold onto the province anyway. In *Philippic* XI.28 Cicero admits that Cassius had no claim on Syria which he calls "another man's province": *cum est in Syriam profectus,* **alienam** *provinciam, si homines legibus scriptis uterentur....* By what right and under what law did Cassius act? *Eo, quod Iuppiter sanxit, ut omnia, quae rei publicae salutaria essent, legitima et iusta haberentur* (*Philippic* XI.28); prime Ciceronian rhetoric, but dangerous in the real world. **insulsus**, -a, -um *tasteless, without wit.* **non insulsus** *witty.* ***cito** (adv.) *quickly, soon.* ***constat** *it is well known, it is an admitted fact.* ***quod** *in that.* **exercitum comparare** *to raise an army.* **nossem = novissem.**

Some Letters of Cicero for Reading at Sight

Ad Atticum III.3

Scr. Itinere circ. Non. Apr. a. 696 (58 B.C.E.).

CICERO ATTICO SAL.

Utinam illum diem videam cum tibi agam gratias quod me vivere coegisti! adhuc quidem valde me paenitet. sed te oro ut ad me Vibonem statim venias quo ego multis de causis converti iter meum. sed eo si veneris, de toto itinere ac fuga mea consilium capere potero. si id non feceris, mirabor; sed confido te esse facturum.

Cicero was banished in the spring of 58 B.C.E. He had considered suicide, but was dissuaded by his friend Atticus. **Vibo** is in the toe of Italy, where Cicero's friend Sicca lived. **utinam** introduces a subjunctive of wish. **adhuc** *still, up to now.* **me paenitet** *I regret.* **statim** *at once.*

Ad Atticum IV.12

Scr. Antii Iun. a. 699 (56 b.c.e.).

CICERO ATTICO SAL.

Egnatius Romae est. sed ego cum eo de re Halimeti vehementer
Antii egi. graviter se acturum cum Aquilio confirmavit. videbis
ergo hominem si voles. Macroni vix videor praesto esse. Idibus
enim auctionem Larini video et biduum praeterea. id tu,
quoniam Macronem tanti facis, ignoscas mihi velim. sed si me
diligis, postridie Kal. cena apud me cum Pilia. prorsus id facies.
Kalendis cogito in hortis Crassipedis quasi in deversorio cenare.
facio fraudem senatus consulto. Inde domum cenatus, ut sim
mane praesto Miloni. ibi te igitur videbo et permanebo. domus te
nostra tota salutat.

L. **Egnatius** Rufus was a business associate of the Cicero brothers. Nothing is
known of the "Halimetus affair" nor what the dealings with Aquilius or Macro
were, though it has been suggested that Atticus wanted Cicero to be Macro's
advocate. **Antii** *at Antium.* **praesto esse** *to be at a person's service.* **Larini:** loc. *at
Larinum.* **et biduum praeterea** *and for two days afterwards.* **tanti:** gen. of value.
ignosco *pardon, forgive.* **postridie Kal.** *on the day after the Kalends* (the 2nd). **Pilia:**
Atticus' wife. **prorsus** (adv.) *by all means.* **Crassipes,** -pedis: Furius Crassipes,
soon to be Tullia's second husband; Cicero is dining at his gardens and has to
postpone his dinner with Atticus. **deversorium** *inn.* **facio fraudem** (+ dat.) *cheat;*
the senatorial decree in question limited expenditures on dining in public places.
domum *homeward;* i.e. he will return home after dinner.

Ad Atticum IV.10

Scr. in Cumano ix Kal. Mai. a. 700 (55 B.C.E.).

CICERO ATTICO SAL.

(1) Puteolis magnus est rumor Ptolomaeum esse in regno. si quid habes certius velim scire. ego hic pascor bibliotheca Fausti. fortasse tu putabas his rebus Puteolanis et Lucrinensibus. ne ista quidem desunt, sed mehercule ut a ceteris oblectationibus deseror et voluptatibus cum propter aetatem tum propter rem publicam, sic litteris sustentor et recreor maloque in illa tua sedecula quam habes sub imagine Aristotelis sedere quam in istorum sella curuli tecumque apud te ambulare quam cum eo quocum video esse ambulandum. sed de illa ambulatione fors viderit aut si qui est qui curet deus.

(2) nostram ambulationem et Laconicum eaque quae circa sunt velim quoad poteris invisas et urgeas Philotimum ut properet, ut possim tibi aliquid in eo genere respondere. Pompeius in Cumanum Parilibus venit. misit ad me statim qui salutem nuntiaret. ad eum postridie mane vadebam, cum haec scripsi.

---

1   **Puteolis** *at Puteoli.* **Ptolomaeus** Ptolemy Auletes who had been deposed in 58 and was now restored by Gabinius, governor of Syria, at Pompey's bidding. **in regno** restored to power [in Egypt]. **pascor** [+ abl.] *feed on.* **Faustus** Cornelius Sulla, son of Sulla the dictator who had brought back a major library from Athens. **rebus Puteolanis et Lucrinensibus** the seafood for which this area (Puteoli and the Lucrine lake) was famous. **mehercule** (interjection) *by Hercules, so help me Hercules.* **cum ... tum** *both ... and.* **malo,** malle, malui *prefer.* **sedecula** (diminutive of *sedes*) *little seat.* **istorum**: the consuls Pompey and Crassus. **sella curulis** *chair of office* used by consuls, praetors, curule aediles. **eo**: Pompey. **si qui** *if any*: with **deus.**

2   **Laconicum** *a steam bath.* **inviso,** -ere (freq. of -video) *come to see, visit.* **Philotimus** a trusted freedman of Terentia's. **respondere** *repay* [his hospitality]. **Cumanum** his Cuman estate. **Parilibus** the *Parilia* on April 21.

Ad Familiares XIV. 20

Scr. de Venusino Kal. Octobribus a.u.c. 707. (October 1, 47 B.C.E.)

TULLIUS S. D. TERENTIAE SUAE

In Tusculanum nos venturos putamus aut Nonis aut postridie:
ibi ut sint omnia parata—plures enim fortasse nobiscum erunt
et, ut arbitror, diutius ibi commorabimur. Labrum si in balineo
non est, ut sit, item cetera, quae sunt ad victum et ad valetudinem
necessaria. Vale. K. Oct. de Venusino.

With **ut sint** and **ut sit**, understand **cura** or **fac. labrum**, -i, n. *basin.* **balineum**, -i,
n. (= balneum) *bath.*

This is the last surviving letter of Cicero to his wife Terentia. In 46 B.C.E. he
divorced her and married his young ward and her substantial fortune. They too
were divorced shortly afterwards.

PART TWO

SELECTIONS FROM SENECA

Lucius Annaeus Seneca's one hundred twenty-four *Epistulae Morales* are not real letters, but short philosophical pieces addressed to a young friend of Seneca's named Gaius Lucilius Iunior, a poet and philosopher who gained success through his energy, talent, and connections. The charm of the Moral Epistles is in the variety of their subjects and in their style which combines brevity of expression, colloquialism, and word play, as well as the studious avoidance of the periodic style best exemplified in Cicero. Quintilian says of him (X.1.129): *Multae in eo claraeque sententiae, multa etiam morum gratia legenda, sed in eloquendo corrupta pleraque, atque eo perniciosissima quod abundant dulcibus vitiis.* "There are many brilliant sententiae in him and many things worth reading for their ethics, but in style much is corrupt and all the more destructive because it is full of appealing faults."

Besides his philosophical work, which includes essays, treatises (under the name *dialogi*), and the twenty books of moral epistles, Seneca wrote the *Apocolocyntosis* (*Pumpkinification*), a satire in prose and verse about the deification of Claudius, and nine tragedies on mythological themes drawn from Greek sources. A tenth, *Octavia*, a tragedy in Roman dress (or *fabula praetexta*) about Nero's wife, is almost universally believed not to be by Seneca.

Dates in Seneca's Life (all dates except birth are C.E.)

Between 4 B.C.E. and 1 C.E. b. in Corduba, Spain.

49   became Nero's tutor.

54   with Burrus became Nero's chief adviser and minister, *amicus principis*.

62   retired from Nero's court and spent the rest of his life writing philosophy.

65   forced to commit suicide after being accused of participation in the failed Pisonian conspiracy (see Tacitus, *Ann.* 15.64).

Despite his being morally compromised by his service to one of history's major villains, Seneca shows himself to be a humane and complex man, perhaps with more talent than he is usually given credit for. What is wrong with the Seneca "letters" as letters? They could be written at any time and to almost anybody. They do not reveal a person at a point in his/her life in relation to another person, though they do occasionally hint at affection for his protegé, Lucilius.

Epistulae Morales 1
Time is of the essence

Seneca Lucilio Suo Salutem

(1) Ita fac, mi Lucili; vindica te tibi, et tempus, quod adhuc aut
auferebatur aut subripiebatur aut excidebat, collige et serva.
Persuade tibi hoc sic esse, ut scribo: quaedam tempora eripiuntur
nobis, quaedam subducuntur, quaedam effluunt. Turpissima
tamen est iactura, quae per neglegentiam fit. Et si volueris
attendere, magna pars vitae elabitur male agentibus, maxima
nihil agentibus, tota vita aliud agentibus.

(2) Quem mihi dabis, qui aliquod pretium tempori ponat,
qui diem aestimet, qui intellegat se cotidie mori? In hoc enim
fallimur, quod mortem prospicimus; magna pars eius iam
praeterit; quicquid aetatis retro est, mors tenet. Fac ergo, mi
Lucili, quod facere te scribis, omnes horas conplectere. Sic fiet, ut
minus ex crastino pendeas, si hodierno manum inieceris. Dum
differtur, vita transcurrit.

Irregular verbs to review: fero (A&G 200), volo (A&G 199), fio (A&G 204), eo,
-ire (A&G 203). Review relative clauses of characteristic (A&G 535); substantive
clauses of result (A&G 568); indirect question (A&G 573-5).

1   **fac**: imperative. dic, duc, fac, and fer / lack the **e** that should be there. **mi**:
vocative of **meus**. Lucili: vocatives of the 2nd declension: -us nouns > -e; -ius
> -i. **vindico** (1) *lay claim to*; *liberate*. **adhuc** adv. *so far, up to now*. **iactura** *a
throwing overboard* [of cargo], *a loss*. **aliud agere** *to do other things*; that is, *to
pay no attention*.

Compound verbs (See appendix II on compounding prefixes): aufero; subripio;
excido (cado); eripio; subduco; effluo; attendere; elabor.

2   **aestimo** (1) *estimate the worth or value of*. **cotidie** (adv.) *daily, every day*.
mori < **morior**. **fallimur** < **fallo** *deceive, mislead*; pass. *be mistaken* **retro**
(adv.) *behind, back*. **conplectere** (imperative) < **complector** *hold in the arms,
embrace, seize, grasp*. **crastinus**, -a, -um *belonging to tomorrow*. **hodierno**
today (neut. or masc. as a noun < **hodiernus** *belonging to today*). **inicio**, -ere,
-ieci, -iectum *throw into*; **manum inicere** *take possession, put one's hand on
property claimed as one's own*. **differo**, -ferre, distuli, dilatum *disperse, put off,
delay*.

Compound verbs: prospicio; praetereo (eo, ire); complector; inicio (iacio); differo;
transcurro.

(3) Omnia, Lucili, aliena sunt, tempus tantum nostrum est. In huius rei unius fugacis ac lubricae possessionem natura nos misit, ex qua expellit quicumque vult. Et tanta stultitia mortalium est, ut quae minima et vilissima sunt, certe reparabilia, imputari sibi, cum impetravere patiantur; nemo se iudicet quicquam debere, qui tempus accepit, cum interim hoc unum est, quod ne gratus quidem potest reddere.

(4) Interrogabis fortasse, quid ego faciam, qui tibi ista praecipio. Fatebor ingenue: quod apud luxuriosum sed diligentem evenit, ratio mihi constat inpensae. Non possum me dicere nihil perdere, sed quid perdam et quare et quemadmodum, dicam; causas paupertatis meae reddam. Sed evenit mihi, quod plerisque non suo vitio ad inopiam redactis; omnes ignoscunt, nemo succurrit.

(5) Quid ergo est? Non puto pauperem, cui quantulumcumque superest, sat est. Tu tamen malo serves tua, et bono tempore incipies. Nam ut visum est maioribus nostris, "sera parsimonia in fundo est." Non enim tantum minimum in imo, sed pessimum remanet. Vale.

3   **alienus, -a, -um** *belonging to another* [> Engl. *alienate*]. **tantum** (adv.) *only*. **lubricus, -a, -um** *slippery* [> Engl. *lubricious*]. **reparabilis, -e** *able to be recovered, retrievable*. **imputor** (1) *to enter as a debt, to charge against a person*. **impetro** (1) *to obtain by request, to succeed in obtaining*. **interim** (adv.) *meanwhile, all the same*.

Compound verbs: expello; imputor; accipio; reddo.

4   **ingenue** (adv.) *frankly, candidly*. **apud** (prep.+ acc.) *near, beside, at the house of, with*. **luxuriosus, -a, -um** *given to self-indulgence, uneconomical*. **ratio constat** *the account balances*. **inpensa, -ae, f.** *expenditure, outlay*.

Compound verbs: interrogo; praecipio *give instructions*; evenio; perdo; reddo *give back, render an account of*; redigo (ago); ignosco *forgive*; succurro *aid, help*.

5   **quantuluscumque** *however small* [an amount]. **malo,** malle, malui (< magis volo) *prefer*. **bono tempore** *in good time, early*. **in fundo** < **fundum** *the bottom*. Proverb: **sera parsimonia in fundo est**: "It's too late to be thrifty when you have reached the bottom" [of your purse or your supplies], see Hesiod, *Works and Days* 369. **non tantum ... sed** [etiam] *not only ... but also*. **in imo** < **imus** *lowest*.

Compound verbs: supersum; incipio; remaneo.

See Appendix II on compounding elements of verbs.

Letter 2: *Epistulae Morales* 31
Strive for the good and avoid the Sirens' songs

SENECA LUCILIO SUO SALUTEM

(1) Agnosco Lucilium meum: incipit quem promiserat exhibere. Sequere illum impetum animi, quo ad optima quaeque calcatis popularibus bonis ibas: non desidero maiorem melioremque te fieri quam moliebaris. Fundamenta tua multum loci occupaverunt: tantum effice quantum conatus es, et illa, quae tecum in animo tulisti, tracta.

(2) Ad summam sapiens eris, si cluseris aures, quibus ceram parum est obdere: firmiore spissamento opus est quam in sociis usum Ulixem ferunt. Illa vox, quae timebatur, erat blanda, non tamen publica: at haec, quae timenda est, non ex uno scopulo, sed ex omni terrarum parte circumsonat. Praetervehere itaque non unum locum insidiosa voluptate suspectum, sed omnes urbes. Surdum te amantissimis tuis praesta: bono animo mala precantur. Et si esse vis felix, deos ora, ne quid tibi ex his quae optantur eveniat.

(3) Non sunt ista bona, quae in te isti volunt congeri: unum bonum est, quod beatae vitae causa et firmamentum est, sibi fidere. Hoc autem contingere non potest, nisi contemptus est labor et in eorum numero habitus, quae neque bona sunt neque mala; fieri enim non potest, ut una ulla res modo mala sit, modo bona, modo levis et perferenda, modo expavescenda. Labor bonum non est: quid ergo est bonum? laboris contemptio.

---

1   *agnosco *recognize.* quem: *i.e.* "the kind of man whom." calco *trample down with the foot.* molior, -iri, molitus/a sum *labor, build up, strive.* occupo (1) *grasp, take possession of.* tracto (1) *freq. of* traho *keep pulling, take in hand, carry out.*

2   *ad summam *as the crowning touch, to sum up, in short.* cera, -ae, f. *wax.* obdo *to place something as a hindrance to* (+ dat.). spissamentum *a means of stopping, a plug.* *opus est (+ abl.) *there is need of.* Ulixes, -is, m. *Ulysses* (Odysseus) referring to the story of the Sirens' song in *Odyssey* 12. *ferunt *they say.* praetervehere: passive imperative. surdus, -a, -um *deaf.*

3   congero *gather together, collect, amass.* firmamentum *support, mainstay.* fido, -ere, fisus/a sum (+ dat.) *trust in , have confidence in.* Labor is not in itself a good, but morally neutral among the *mediae res.* modo ... modo *at one time ... at another time.* expavesco, -ere, -avi *become frightened, take fright.*

(4) Itaque in vanum operosos culpaverim: rursus ad honesta
nitentes, quanto magis incubuerint minusque sibi vinci ac
strigare permiserint, admirabor et clamabo, "tanto melior,
surge et inspira et clivum istum uno, si potes, spiritu exsupera."
Generosos animos labor nutrit.

(5) Non est ergo quod ex illo voto vetere parentum tuorum
eligas, quid contingere tibi velis, quid optes; et in totum iam per
maxima acto viro turpe est etiamnunc deos fatigare. Quid votis
opus est? fac te ipse felicem; facies autem, si intellexeris bona esse,
quibus admixta virtus est, turpia, quibus malitia coniuncta est.
Quemadmodum sine mixtura lucis nihil splendidum est, nihil
atrum, nisi quod tenebras habet aut aliquid in se traxit obscuri,
quemadmodum sine adiutorio ignis nihil calidum est, nihil sine
aere frigidum, ita honesta et turpia virtutis ac malitiae societas
efficit.

(6) Quid ergo est bonum? rerum scientia. Quid malum est?
rerum imperitia. Ille prudens atque artifex pro tempore quaeque
repellet aut eliget; sed nec quae repellit timet nec miratur quae
eligit, si modo magnus illi et invictus animus est. Summitti te ac
deprimi veto. Laborem si non recuses, parum est: posce.

(7) "Quid ergo?" inquis "labor frivolus et supervacuus et quem
humiles causae evocaverunt non est malus?" Non magis quam
ille, qui pulchris rebus impenditur, quoniam animi est ipsa
tolerantia, quae se ad dura et aspera hortatur ac dicit, "quid
cessas? non est viri timere sudorem."

---

4   **culpaverim**: potential subjunctive. ***nitor**, -i, nisus/a sum *support, strain,*
     struggle, strive. **incubo** *lie on, throw oneself on*. **strigo** *to come to a standstill*
     (originally an agricultural term). **tanto melior** (es)

5   ***non est ... quod** *there is no reason that/why*. **votum**, -i, n. *vow* [cf. *ex voto*].
     eligo *pull out, pick out*. **in totum** *in general, altogether*. **per maxima** *through*
     the highest offices. **acto viro**: dat. **fatigo** (1) *tire out, weary, worry, plague*.
     quemadmodum *in what way, in the manner in which, as*.

6   **imperitia**, -ae, f. *lack of skill, ignorance*. **pro tempore** *in accordance with the*
     needs of the moment. **summitti ac deprimi** *to be brought down and reduced*.
     recuso (1) *protest, reject*.

7   **supervacuus**, -a, -um *in excess, redundant, unnecessary*. **impendo** *pay out,*
     devote, expend. **viri**: predicate gen. of characteristic: gen. + **est** *belongs to*.
     sudor, -oris, m. *sweat*.

(8) Huc et illud accedat, ut perfecta virtus sit, aequalitas ac tenor vitae per omnia consonans sibi, quod non potest esse, nisi rerum scientia contingit et ars, per quam humana ac divina noscantur. Hoc est summum bonum; quod si occupas, incipis deorum socius esse, non supplex.

(9) "Quomodo" inquis "isto pervenitur?" Non per Poeninum Graiumve montem nec per deserta Candaviae; nec Syrtes tibi nec Scylla aut Charybdis adeundae sunt, quae tamen omnia transisti procuratinculae pretio: tutum iter est, iucundum est, ad quod natura te instruxit. Dedit tibi illa, quae si non deserueris, par deo surges.

(10) Parem autem te deo pecunia non faciet: deus nihil habet. Praetexta non faciet: deus nudus est. Fama non faciet nec ostentatio tui et in populos nominis dimissa notitia: nemo novit deum, multi de illo male existimant, et impune. Non turba servorum lecticam tuam per itinera urbana ac peregrina portantium: deus ille maximus potentissimusque ipse vehit omnia. Ne forma quidem et vires beatum te facere possunt: nihil horum patitur vetustatem.

8   **tenor,** -oris, m. *sustained course.* **ars per quam** = philosophy.
9   **Poeninus** -a, -um *Pennine* (of the Alps from Mont Blanc to Monte Rosa). **Graius**, -a, -um [Greek] *Graius mons* the little St. Bernard Pass and surrounding mountains. **Candavia** a mountain in Illyria. **Syrtes**, -is, f. the desert regions on the north coast of Africa, between Carthage and Cyrene, known for treacherous quick-sand. **adeundae** < **adeo**, -ire.

   procuratincula *a petty procuratorship.* **deserueris** < **desero** *part company with, fail, leave in the lurch.* **surgo**, -ere, surrexi, -rectum *rise, emerge.*
10 **praetexta (toga)** *a toga with a purple border* worn by Senators. **lectica**, -ae, f. *a litter.*

(11) Quaerendum est quod non fiat in dies eius, cui non possit
obstari. Quid hoc est? animus, sed hic rectus, bonus, magnus.
Quid aliud voces hunc quam deum in corpore humano
hospitantem? Hic animus tam in equitem Romanum quam in
libertinum, quam in servum potest cadere. Quid est enim eques
Romanus aut libertinus aut servus? nomina ex ambitione aut
iniuria nata. Subsilire in caelum ex angulo licet: exsurge modo

> et te quoque dignum
> finge deo.

Finges autem non auro vel argento: non potest ex hac materia
imago deo exprimi similis; cogita illos, cum propitii essent,
fictiles fuisse. Vale.

---

11   **eius**: another reading is **peius**. * **obsto**, -are, -stiti, -statum *meet face to face,*
stand in the way of, oppose. **angulus**, -i, m. *angle, corner, narrow space.* **et te**
quoque dignum/ finge deo: Vergil, *Aeneid* VIII. 364-5. **propitius**, -a, -um
favorably inclined, well-disposed. **fictilis** *made of clay.*

PART THREE

SELECTIONS FROM PLINY'S LETTERS

Gaius Plinius Caecilius Secundus (known as Pliny the Younger), because of the times he lived in and possibly also because of the manner of man he was, had a less momentous political, professional, and literary life than Cicero. Still, he had a respectable career as a pleader, specializing in cases concerned with property, and went through all the offices of the imperial *cursus honorum*, ending his career and his life in service to the emperor as imperial legate to Bithynia. The first nine books of his letters, probably written between 97 and 109 C.E., give a varied picture of the life and interests of cultured Romans of the period. They reveal a personality at once generous and vain and a style both simple and artificial. He was a man of strong affections who deeply loved his wife and shows genuine admiration for many women as well as men. He betrays anxiety about his writing, a need to be productive, and a concern to do the right thing. The letters of book ten to Trajan and Trajan's rescripts are a unique set of documents illuminating provincial government in imperial times.

Major events in Pliny's life (all dates are C.E.)

61/62 b. at Comum (IV.13)
His father died when he was young, and he was under the
guardianship of Verginius Rufus.

79 the destruction of Vesuvius and death of Pliny the Elder (III.5, VI.20).
Pliny the Elder adopted him in his will.

ca. 80 began his career as a pleader.

100 consul suffectus, delivered *Panegyricus* in honor of Trajan.
After his consulship married Calpurnia (VI.4, VI.7).

111-114? Legate to Bithynia; letters, book X; died (probably in Bithynia).

Letter 1, Book I. 1
Introduction to Pliny's Letters and Life

C. PLINIUS SEPTICIO SUO S.

Frequenter hortatus es ut epistulas, si quas paulo curatius scripsissem, colligerem publicaremque. Collegi non servato temporis ordine (neque enim historiam componebam), sed ut quaeque in manus venerat. Superest ut nec te consilii nec me paeniteat obsequii. Ita enim fiet ut eas quae adhuc neglectae iacent requiram, et si quas addidero, non supprimam. Vale.

C. Plinius Septicio suo S.: the formula for addressing a letter: see introduction page 6.

This is the opening letter of the collection and the dedication of the book. Its importance lies in the fact that it is an explanation of the reasons for and method of publishing this and the following books of letters and has been useful to scholars in establishing the chronology of the letters and books.

Septicius Clarus was an equestrian of Pliny's generation who later rose to the praetorian prefecture under Hadrian, c. 119 C.E. By dedicating the book to Clarus, as Sherwin-White notes, Pliny avoided offending any senator. The other books do not begin with such introductions.

Review: deponent verbs (Appendix D and A&G 190-2); jussive noun clauses (Appendix C; A&G 563); indefinite pronouns: quisque, siquis (Appendix B); substantive clauses of result (A&G 567-8); impersonals and genitive of object of feeling (A&G 207-8, 354b).

* **hortor**, -ari, hortatus/a sum *urge, exhort.* **epistulas, siquas paulo curatius scripsissem**: see introduction page 2. * **paulo** (adv.) *a little, somewhat.* **collegi non servato temporis ordine ... sed ut quaeque in manus venerat ...** this is not entirely true; most of the books belong to a particular time period, though each book contains various kinds of letters and is arranged in part with diversity of subject matter in mind. * **supersum**, -esse, -fui *be left, remain.* * **paenitet**, -ere, -uit *regret*: impersonal verb with accusative of the person who feels regret and genitive of the thing which causes the regret. **me paenitet** *I regret.* * **obsequium**, -i, n. *compliance.*

Letter 2, Book I. 3
Life in the Country

C. PLINIUS CANINIO RUFO SUO S.

(1) Quid agit Comum, tuae meaeque deliciae? quid suburbanum amoenissimum? Quid illa porticus verna semper? quid platanon opacissimus? quid euripus viridis et gemmeus? quid subiectus et serviens lacus? quid illa mollis et tamen solida gestatio? quid balineum illud, quod plurimus sol implet et circumit? quid triclinia

---

Address: **Caninius Rufus**, a wealthy landowner in Pliny's native Comum (modern day Como) who avoided the hustle and bustle of Rome and seems to have been preoccupied with his own affairs. This is the first of seven letters to Caninius Rufus. Six of them concern literature and three encourage Caninius to work seriously on a masterpiece of his own; by the ninth book Caninius has produced something.

Thematic parallells of nature and death and the passage of one's home to heir after heir are common in Latin.

Review: gerundives (A&G 504-7); jussive subjunctive (both dependent and independent subjunctive, Appendix C; A&G 439, 563); indirect question (A&G 574); relative clauses of characteristic (A&G 535); genitive of price/value (a subcategory of the genitive of quality or description, A&G 345, 417)

1   * **quid agit Comum**? Pliny personifies Comum (present day Como) and all the other items in a list of clauses/phrases beginning with **quid**. The idiom usually appears as **quid agis** *what's up with you?* Lit. *what are you doing?* * **deliciae**, -arum, f. pl. *pet, favorite* [cf. Catullus' *passer, deliciae meae puellae*]. **suburbanus**, -a, -um *near the city*; **suburbanum**, -i, n. *a country place close to the city*. ***amoenus**, -a, -um *pleasant, beautiful*. [> Engl. *amenity*.] **porticus**, -us, f. = Greek *stoa*: *a walk covered by a roof, supported on columns*. **vernus**, -a, -um *occurring in spring, as in spring, spring* [> Engl. *vernal*]. **platanon**, -onis, m. [Greek] *grove of plane trees*. **opacus**, -a, -um *shady, sheltered from heat and sun*. **euripus** -i, m. [Greek] *canal, water-course*. **viridis**, -e *green*. **gemmeus**, -a, -um *set with precious stones; jewelled, sparkling*. **subiectus et serviens lacus** "the pleasant lake lying below": Lacus Larius, now called Lake Como, or possibly a man-made pool. **gestatio**, -onis, f. *promenade*; literally a *bearing* or *carrying* [from *gero*]: the meaning is transferred from the activity to "the place where one is carried to get some fresh air." **balineum (balneum)**, -i, n. *suite of bathing rooms, bath*. **impleo**, -ere, -evi, -etum *fill*. **circumit** < circumeo, -ire, -ii, -itum *go around, surround*. * **triclinium**, -ii, n. [Greek], *a couch running around three sides of a table for reclining at meals* > *a dining room*.

illa popularia, illa paucorum? quid cubicula diurna, nocturna?

(2) Possident te et per vices partiuntur? an, ut solebas, intentione rei familiaris obeundae crebris excursionibus avocaris? Si te possident, felix beatusque es; si minus, unus ex multis.

(3) Quin tu (tempus est enim) humiles et sordidas curas aliis mandas et ipse te in alto isto pinguique secessu studiis adseris? Hoc sit negotium tuum, hoc otium, hic labor, haec quies: in his vigilia, in his etiam somnus reponatur.

(4) Effinge aliquid et exclude quod sit perpetuo tuum. Nam reliqua rerum tuarum post te alium atque alium dominum sortientur, hoc numquam tuum desinet esse, si semel coeperit.

(5) Scio quem animum, quod horter ingenium. Tu modo enitere ut tibi ipse sis tanti quanti videberis aliis si tibi fueris. Vale.

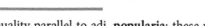

paucorum: gen. of quality parallel to adj. **popularia**; these would be dining rooms for grand parties and for more intimate dinners. * **cubiculum**, -i, n. "an appartment for reclining or for sleeping" [i.e. a *bedroom*] < cubo "to lie down/sleep". **diurnus**, -a, -um *during the day, for daytime use*. **nocturnus**, -a, -um *during the night, for nighttime use*.

2   * **vicis** [genitive, no nominative] *change, alternation, turn*; **per vices** *by turns*. **partio/partior** *share, divide*. **an** (conj.) *or*, introducing the second part of a double question. **intentio**, -onis, f. *stretching > exertion, effort*; **intentione**: abl. of cause. * **res familiaris** *one's estate, property*. * **obeo**, -ire, -ii, -itum *go/come to; engage in, attend to, discharge, perform*. **rei familiaris obeundae**: gerundive construction depending on *intentione*. **creber**, -bra, -brum *frequent, repeated*. **excursio**, -onis, f. *a running back and forth, expedition*. * **si minus** *if not*. **unus ex multis** *like the rest of us*.

3   * **quin** *why not*? **altus**, -a, -um *high, deep*. **pinguis**, -e *fat, rich, comfortable, luxurious*. **secessus**, -us, m. *a going away, withdrawal; retreat, recess*. * **adsero** -ere, -ui, -tum [a legal term] "to declare a slave to be free, to appropriate something, to declare one to belong to something." The usual construction is "to declare something to belong to oneself" but here Pliny suggests that his friend sentence himself to belonging to his *studia*. Legal and technical business terms are frequent in Pliny. **vigilia**, -ae, f. *wakefulness, hours awake*.

4   **effingo**, -ere, -finxi, -fictum *form, express*. **excludo**, -ere, -clusi, -clusum *cut off, hatch, bring out*. **perpetuo** (adv.) *constantly, forever*. **sortior**, -iri, -itus/a sum *draw lots, obtain by lot, have allocated*. **desino**, -ere, -ivi, -itum *cease, leave off*. **semel** (adv.) *once*.

5   **enitor**, -i, -nixus/nisus/a sum *struggle, exert oneself, strive*. **tanti ... quanti**: gen. of price, value. **videberis ... si fueris**: future more vivid condition.

Letter 3: Book III. 5
Pliny the Elder's modus vivendi

C. Plinius Baebio Macro Suo S.

(1) Pergratum est mihi quod tam diligenter libros avunculi mei lectitas ut habere omnes velis quaerasque qui sint omnes.

(2) Fungar indicis partibus atque etiam quo sint ordine scripti notum tibi faciam: est enim haec quoque studiosis non iniucunda cognitio.

(3) *De iaculatione equestri* unus: hunc, cum praefectus alae militaret, pari ingenio curaque conposuit. *De vita Pomponi Secundi* duo; a quo singulariter amatus hoc memoriae amici quasi debitum munus exsolvit.

Baebius Macer, a senator, curator of the Appian Way, Prefect of the City (see Martial 10.18, 12.98).

Review result clauses (A&G 537); indirect question (A&G 574); future conditions (A&G 516); gerunds (501-7).

1   **pergratus, -a, -um**: the prefix **per-** = *through, thoroughly, very.* *quod *the fact that.* **lectito** (1): frequentative of **lego**, *gather eagerly,* or *read often, avidly, with attention.* Frequentatives are usually formed from the perfect passive participle and indicate an intensified action.

2   *fungor, -i, functus/a sum *discharge, be engaged* (+ abl.). **fungar indicis partibus** "I shall perform the role of an index." **studiosus, -a, -um**: the suffix **-osus** means "full of".

3   *De iaculatione equestri* **unus** "On throwing from a horse", one book (probably written before 50 c.e.). The numbers beside the titles of the works indicate how many books. **praefectus alae** "prefect of a regiment" [lit., *wing*]. **Pomponius Secundus** wrote poetry and plays and, though booed by his audience, was admired by the emperor Claudius, who made him consul and later governor of Upper Germany. **singulariter** (adv.) *in particular, exceedingly.* **hoc** refers to the book, but takes its gender from **munus. exsolvo**, -ere, -solvi, -solutum *loose, deliver, pay.*

(4) *Bellorum Germaniae* viginti; quibus omnia quae cum
Germanis gessimus bella collegit. Incohavit, cum in Germania
militaret, somnio monitus: adstitit ei quiescenti Drusi Neronis
effigies, qui Germaniae latissime victor ibi periit, commendabat
memoriam suam orabatque ut se ab iniuria oblivionis adsereret.

(5) *Studiosi* tres, in sex volumina propter amplitudinem divisi,
quibus oratorem ab incunabulis instituit et perficit. *Dubii
sermonis* octo: scripsit sub Nerone novissimis annis, cum omne
studiorum genus paulo liberius et erectius periculosum servitus
fecisset.

(6) *A fine Aufidi Bassi* triginta unus. *Naturae historiarum* triginta
septem, opus diffusum, eruditum, nec minus varium quam ipsa
natura.

4   ***Bellorum Germaniae*** on the wars in Germany under Caesar, Augustus, and
Tiberius and a possible source for Tacitus' treatment of events in Germany in
Ann. 1-6. **incoho**/inchoo (1) *begin* (> Engl. *inchoate*). ***somnium**, -i, n. *dream*.
Drusus Nero: father of Claudius the emperor, in command in Germany from
12 to 9 B.C.E. **effigies** (no gen.), f. *likeness, image*. **adsereret** "that he vindicate
him from..." * **adsero** -ere, -ui, -tum [a legal term] "to declare a slave to be
free", "to appropriate something."

5   ***Studiosi* tres** *The Scholar* in three volumes; a rhetorical handbook quoted by
Quintilian and Aulus Gellius. **ab incunabulis** *from the cradle*; lit. "from swaddling
clothes" [cf. Engl. *incunabulum*, an early printed book, from before 1501.] ***Dubii
sermonis*** works on bad grammar, diction, or usage published before 68 C.E.; in
NH pref. 28 Pliny refers to them as *libellos de grammatica*. **novissimis annis** *in
the last years*. **erectius** *more lofty, elevated, ambitious* (compar. adj. of **erectus**
perf. pass. participle of **erigo**). **servitus**, -tutis, f. *slavery, servitude*: the period
after the Pisonian conspiracy of 66 (see Tacitus, *Ann.* 15.50).

6   ***A fine Aufidi Bassi***: Pliny (*NH pref.* 20) calls this "a history of our times."
Aufidius Bassus: historian who covered the period from the death of Caesar
to the later years of Claudius. Pliny took up from the end of the Claudian
regime through the Flavians. ***Naturae historiarum* triginta septem**: the
famous *Naturalis Historia* has survived.

(7) Miraris quod tot volumina multaque in his tam scrupulosa homo occupatus absolverit? magis miraberis, si scieris illum aliquandiu causas actitasse, decessisse anno sexto quinquagesimo, medium tempus distentum impeditumque qua officiis maximis qua amicitia principum egisse.

(8) Sed erat acre ingenium, incredibile studium, summa vigilantia. Lucubrare Vulcanalibus incipiebat, non auspicandi causa sed studendi, statim a nocte multa, hieme vero ab hora septima, vel cum tardissime, octava, saepe sexta. Erat sane somni paratissimi, non numquam etiam inter ipsa studia instantis et deserentis.

(9) Ante lucem ibat ad Vespasianum imperatorem (nam ille quoque noctibus utebatur), inde ad delegatum sibi officium. Reversus domum, quod relicum temporis, studiis reddebat.

---

7   **scrupulosa** "requiring great care," "full of minute detail," an apt description of the encyclopedic *Natural Histories*, which Gian Biaggio Conte in *Genres and Readers* (tr. by Glenn W. Most, Baltimore and London: Johns Hopkins University Press, 1994) calls "the inventory of the world" (the sub-heading of his chapter). Pliny seems almost to be imitating in miniature his uncle's massive work, which is full of lists and numbers; as Conte writes: "in the *Naturalis historia* even the most minute things are customarily enumerated and absolutely everything is catalogued" (67). **homo occupatus**: Pliny the Elder served in the military in Germany, held at least one procuratorship, and under Vespasian and Titus was prefect of the fleet of Misenum until his death. **absolvo, -ere, -solvi, -solutum** *discharge, complete.* **scieris**: fut. perf. **aliquandiu** *for a while, for some time.* **actitasse** = agitavisse < **actito** *plead.* **decedo, -ere, -cessi, -cessum** *depart, die.* **distentum impeditumque** *busy and bogged down.* **qua ... qua** *as well ... as.* **amicitia principum** refers to his role of adviser to the emperors (Vespasian and Titus); though not an official position, we could compare this to a cabinet post.

8   **acre ingenium ... summa vigilantia**: add **ei**, dat. of possession: nom. + est/erat + dat. = he/she had. **lucubro** (1) *work by lamplight.* **Vulcanalibus** *the festival of Vulcan,* August 23. **auspicor** (1) *take the auspices.* ***statim** (adv.) *regularly, at once.* **a multa nocte** "from deep in the night" ***hiems, -is,** f. *winter.* **sexta** [hora] *midnight;* **septima** *the first hour after midnight;* **octava** *the second hour after midnight.* **somni paratissimi**: *gen. of characteristic. ***non numquam** (adv.) *sometimes.* **instantis et deserentis**: genitives with **somni**. **insto, -are** *stand in, press upon.* **desero** *leave, abandon.*

9   **delego** (1) *assign.* ***revertor, -i, -versus/a sum** *come back, return.* ***domum** *home* (acc. of place to which). **relicum** = reliquum.

(10) Post cibum saepe, quem interdiu levem et facilem veterum more sumebat, aestate, si quid otii, iacebat in sole, liber legebatur, adnotabat excerpebatque. Nihil enim legit quod non excerperet: dicere etiam solebat nullum esse librum tam malum ut non aliqua parte prodesset.

(11) Post solem plerumque frigida lavabatur; deinde gustabat dormiebatque minimum: mox quasi alio die studebat in cenae tempus. Super hanc liber legebatur, adnotabatur, et quidem cursim.

(12) Memini quendam ex amicis, cum lector quaedam perperam pronuntiasset, revocasse et repeti coegisse, huic avunculum meum dixisse "intellexeras nempe?" cum ille adnuisset, "Cur ergo revocabas? decem amplius versus hac tua interpellatione perdidimus."

(13)Tanta erat parsimonia temporis. Surgebat aestate a cena luce, hieme intra primam noctis, et tamquam aliqua lege cogente. Haec inter medios labores urbisque fremitum.

(14) In secessu solum balinei tempus studiis eximebatur: cum dico "balinei" de interioribus loquor; nam dum destringitur tergiturque, audiebat aliquid aut dictabat.

---

10   **cibus, -i,** m. *food, meal.* **interdiu** "during the day". **facilem** *simple, easy* [easy on the system and/or easily prepared]. **veterum more**: abl. of manner [cf. *mos maiorum*]. ***aestas, -tatis,** f. *summer;* **aestate** *in summer.* **si quid**: after si, nisi, num, and ne *quis/quid = aliquid/quid.* **otii**: partitive gen. **liber legebatur**: like many upper class Romans, Pliny employed a reader (*lector*), very likely a slave or freedman. **excerpo, -ere, -cerpsi, -cerptum** *extract, make selections.* ***prosum,** prodesse, profui *be useful.*

11   **plerumque** (adv.) *for the most part.* **frigida**: supply **aqua.** **mox** (adv.) *afterward.* **cenae tempus**: *dinnertime* was in mid- to late afternoon (around 3 or 4 p.m.). **cursim** (adv.) *quickly, hastily.*

12   **perperam** (adv.) *incorrectly.* ***nempe** *indeed*: used in questions to ask for a more precise and emphatic statement of something already said: "oh, really?" ***adnuo, -ere, -nui** *nod in agreement, nod assent.* **interpellatio, -onis,** f. *interruption.*

13   **luce**: *while it was still light.* **primam [horam] noctis. fremitus, -us,** m. *hum, rumble, roar, noise.*

14   **in secessu** "on vacation." ***balineum, -i,** n. *bath.* **eximo, -ere, -imi, -emptum** *take away.* **de interioribus** refers to the time actually spent in the water. **destringo, -ere, -nxi, -nctum** *strip off, scrub down.* **tergo, -ere, tersi, tersum** *wipe dry.*

(15) In itinere quasi solutus ceteris curis huic uni vacabat: ad latus notarius cum libro et pugillaribus, cuius manus hieme manicis muniebantur, ut ne caeli quidem asperitas ullum studiis tempus eriperet; qua ex causa Romae quoque sella vehebatur.

(16) Repeto me correptum ab eo cur ambularem: "poteras" inquit "has horas non perdere"; nam perire omne tempus arbitrabatur quod studiis non impenderetur.

(17) Hac intentione tot ista volumina peregit electorumque commentarios centum sexaginta mihi reliquit, opisthographos quidem et minutissime scriptos; qua ratione multiplicatur hic numerus. Referebat ipse potuisse se, cum procuraret in Hispania, vendere hos commentarios Largio Licino quadringentis milibus nummum, et tunc aliquanto pauciores erant.

(18) Nonne videtur tibi recordanti quantum legerit, quantum scripserit, nec in officiis ullis nec in amicitia principis fuisse, rursus, cum audis quid studiis laboris inpenderit, nec scripsisse satis nec legisse? Quid est enim quod non aut illae occupationes inpedire aut haec instantia non possit efficere?

---

15 ***quasi** *as if.* **vaco** (1) *be free* (for + dat.). **notarius**, -i, m. *note-taker, shorthand writer.* **pugillaria**, n.pl. *notebooks* (from **pugillus** [> Engl. pugilist] *handful* < **pugnus** *fist*). **manicis**: "with mittens," i.e. the sleeves of the tunic were lengthened to pull down around the hands. **munio**, -ire, -ivi, -itum *fortify* (< **moenia** *wall*). ***ne ... quidem** *not ... even.*

16 **repeto me correptum ... cur** "I recall that I was scolded [with the question] ... why." **inquit** < **inquam** (defective verb) *say*: used in direct quotations [cf. Engl. *quoth*]. **impendo**, -ere, -pendi, -pensum *spend.*

17 **intentio**, -onis, f. *application.* **perago**, -ere, -egi, -actum *go through.* **commentarii**, -orum, m.pl. *notebooks.* **opisthographos** "written on the back" (a Greek word); rolls were usually not written on the back. ***refero**, -ferre, rettuli, -latum *bring back, recount.* **cum procuraret** "when he was procurator." **Larcius Licinus**: an orator, governor of Hispania Terraconensis. **quadrigentis milibus**: abl. of price ("for"). **nummum**: archaic gen. pl. of **nummus**, -i, m. a *sesterce.* **tunc = tum. aliquanto** (adv.) *considerably, somewhat.*

18 In this section find an indirect question, an indirect statement, a relative clause of characteristic. **recordor** (1) *think over.* **rursus** (adv.) *again.* **instantia**, -ae, f. *perseverance.*

(19) Itaque soleo ridere, cum me quidam studiosum vocant, qui,
si comparer illi, sum desidiosissimus. Ego autem tantum, quem
partim publica partim amicorum officia distringunt? quis ex
istis qui tota vita litteris adsident collatus illi non quasi somno et
inertiae deditus erubescat?

(20) Extendi epistulam, cum hoc solum quod requirebas
scribere destinassem, quos libros reliquisset: confido tamen haec
quoque tibi non minus grata quam ipsos libros futura, quae
te non tantum ad legendos eos verum etiam ad simile aliquid
elaborandum possunt aemulationis stimulis excitare. Vale.

19 **desidiosus, -a, -um** *lazy.* **ego autem** ... a sentence fragment; some predicate
must be understood from the previous line. **tantum** (adv.) *only.* **partim** (adv.)
in part. **publica [officia]** parallel and in contrast to **amicorum. distringo,**
-ere, -nxi, -nctum *distract the attention of.* **tota vita:** abl. of duration of time
(usually expressed by the acc.): this is an extension of the abl. of time within
which, with the implication that the event or activity extended over the whole
period (A&G 424b); this construction becomes more common in the "Silver
Age." **assideo, -ere, -sedi, -sessum** *sit by, devote oneself to* (+ dat.). **dedo,**
-ere, -didi, -ditum *give up, surrender.* **erubesco, -ere, -rubui** *blush;* **erubescat:**
potential subjunctive. **collatus illi** *compared to him.*

20 In this section find a **cum**-concessive (*although*) clause, an indirect question,
a dative with adjective, an indirect statement, two gerundives of purpose.
destino (1) *make firm, resolve to.* **confido, -ere, -fisus/a sum** *trust, believe.*
futura [esse] in indirect statement. **non ... tantum ... verum etiam** (= **non**
solum ... sed etiam) *not only ... but also.* **aemulatio, -onis,** f. *rivalry, competition*
[> Engl. *emulation*]. **stimulus, -i,** m. *goad.*

Letter 4: *Epistulae* VI.20
Pliny and his mother survive the eruption of Vesuvius

C. PLINIUS TACITO SUO S.

(1) Ais te adductum litteris quas exigenti tibi de morte avunculi mei scripsi cupere cognoscere quos ego Miseni relictus (id enim ingressus abruperam) non solum metus verum etiam casus pertulerim. "Quamquam animus meminisse horret, incipiam."

(2)Profecto avunculo ipse reliquum tempus studiis (ideo enim remanseram) inpendi: mox balineum, cena, somnus inquietus et brevis.

Tacito Suo: Tacitus: the famous historian. The date is August 24. Pliny describes his own and his mother's experiences at Misenum, while his uncle Pliny the Elder was at Stabiae. Tacitus had written to Pliny to request an account of the death of the elder Pliny in the eruption of Vesuvius, which destroyed Pompeii, Herculaneum, and many settlements along the Bay of Naples on August 23-24, 79 C.E. Pliny's answer was the famous *Ep.* VI.16, the eyewitness description of the cloud rising from Vesuvius, the departure of Pliny the Elder for a closer look and to help the people of Stabiae, and the report from witnesses of his subsequent demise. The younger Pliny has a narrative and descriptive style as riveting as any in the Roman world. In this letter, written again at Tacitus' urging, he takes up where he left off in VI.16, coyly beginning the narrative of his own adventures, *Interim Miseni ego et mater–sed nihil ad historiam, nec tu aliud quam de exitu eius scire voluisti. Finem ergo faciam.* "Meanwhile at Misenum mother and I–but that has nothing to do with history and you requested information only about his death. So I shall end here."

Review deponent verbs (Appendix D and A&G 190-2); conditions contrary to fact (A&G 517).

1   **ais** *you say*: defective verb: other present forms *****aio, ait, aiunt. exigenti** with **tibi** < **exigo**, -ere, -egi, -actum *drive out, exact, demand, call for*. **id ... ingressus** "after setting out on that [topic]." See the end of letter VI.16 quoted above. **quos**: with **metus** and **casus**: introduces an indirect question; **metus**, -us, m. *fear*. **Miseni**: *at Misenum*, the major naval station on the west coast, on a promontory of the bay of Baiae. The elder Pliny was prefect of the fleet of Misenum. **Quamquam animus meminisse horret, incipiam**: a quotation from Vergil, *Aeneid* II. 12.

2   *****proficiscor**, -i, profectus/a sum *set out*. *****ideo** *for that reason*: in *Ep.* VI.16.7 Pliny's uncle invites him to come along in his investigation of the phenomenon but he writes: *respondi studere me malle*. *****mox** as is usual in Silver Age Latin, *afterward, next*.

(3) Praecesserat per multos dies tremor terrae minus formidulosus quia Campaniae solitus. Illa vero nocte ita invaluit ut non moveri omnia sed verti crederentur.

(4) Inrumpit cubiculum meum mater: surgebam, invicem, si quiesceret, excitaturus. Residimus in area domus, quae mare a tectis modico spatio dividebat.

(5) Dubito constantiam vocare an inprudentiam debeam; agebam enim duodevicesimum annum: posco librum Titi Livi et quasi per otium lego atque etiam, ut coeperam, excerpo. Ecce, amicus avunculi, qui nuper ad eum ex Hispania venerat, ut me et matrem sedentes, me vero etiam legentem videt, illius patientiam, securitatem meam corripit: nihilo segnius ego intentus in librum.

(6) Iam hora diei prima, et adhuc dubius et quasi languidus dies. Iam quassatis circumiacentibus tectis, quamquam in aperto loco, angusto tamen, magnus et certus ruinae metus.

---

3   **formidulosus**, -a, -um *causing fear.* **Campaniae solitus** *usual for Campania, common in Campania.* **invalesco**, -ere, invalui *become strong.* **verti = everti**.

4   **cubiculum**, -i, n. *bedroom.* **invicem** (adv.) *in turn.* **excitaturus** fut. act. ptcpl. expressing purpose. **resido**, -ere, -sedi *sit down, settle.* **area**, -ae, f. *an open courtyard,* outside the house. ***tectum**, -i, n. *roof, house.*

5   ***an** *or:* introduces the second member of a double question. **agebam ... duodevicesimum annum**: this line dates Pliny's birth. **posco**, -ere, poposci *demand, call for.* **per otium** *at leisure*; **per** with expressions implying time means *during a time of.* ***ut** + indicative *as, when.* **ecce** *look, here.* Pliny announces the arrival of this new character to invite the reader into the scene, as if he is right there in front of us. Pliny the Elder had been procurator in Spain. **illius** that is, **matris. corripit** *chides, scolds*: Pliny uses the present (called historical or narrative present) for dramatic effect. **segnius** *more slowly, sluggishly*; **nihilo/non/haud segnius** *none the slower, with undiminished zeal.* **ego intentus [sum]** Pliny leaves out the forms of **esse**, again for immediacy.

6ff. Supply "it was," "we were," or "there was" throughout.

6   ***adhuc** (adv.) *until now.* **languidus**, -a, -um *faint, half-hearted, sick.* Pliny personifies **dies** as a living thing, whether plant or animal. **quasso**, -are, -avi, -atum *shake, shatter.* **circumiaceo** *surround* < ***iaceo**, -ere *lie.* ***apertus**, -a, -um *open.* **angustus**, -a, -um *narrow.* **ruina**, -ae, f. *downfall, catastrophe.*

(7) Tum demum excedere oppido visum: sequitur vulgus attonitum, quodque in pavore simile prudentiae, alienum consilium suo praefert ingentique agmine abeuntis premit et inpellit.

(8) Egressi tecta consistimus. Multa ibi miranda, multas formidines patimur. Nam vehicula quae produci iusseramus, quamquam in planissimo campo, in contrarias partes agebantur ac ne lapidibus quidem fulta in eodem vestigio quiescebant.

(9) Praeterea mare in se resorberi et tremore terrae quasi repelli videbamus. Certe processerat litus multaque animalia maris siccis harenis detinebat. Ab altero latere nubes atra et horrenda ignei spiritus tortis vibratisque discursibus rupta in longas flammarum figuras dehiscebat: fulguribus illae et similes et maiores erant.

7   ***demum** (adv.) *at last, finally.* ***oppidum**, -i, n. *town, collection of houses.* ***visum [est]** *it seemed best.* ***sequor**, -i, secutus/a sum *follow.* ***vulgus**, -i, n. *crowd, mob.* **attonitus**, -a, -um *thunderstruck, confounded* [> *astonished*]. **pavor**, -oris, m. *terror, panic.* **prudentiae:** dat. with **similis.** ***alienus**, -a, -um *belonging to another.* ***ingens**, -entis (adj.) *huge.* ***agmen**, -inis, n. *line of march, multitude.* **abeuntis:** masc./fem. acc. pl. participle "those going away" < ***abeo**, -ire, -ii/-ivi, -itum.

8   **egressi tecta** "after getting past the houses." **consisto**, -ere, -stiti, -stitum *come to a stop.* **formido**, -inis, f. *fear, terror.* ***patior**, pati, passus/a sum *suffer, experience.* **vehiculum**, -i, n. *carriage, conveyance.* ***quamquam** (conj.) *although.* **planus**, -a, -um *even, flat.* **campus**, -i, m. *field, open country, level land.* **fulcio**, -ire, fulsi, fultum *prop, support;* **fulta** agrees with **vehicula.**

9   ***praeterea** *besides.* **resorbeo** *suck back, swallow again.* **litus**, -oris, n. *shoreline, coast* [> Engl. *littoral*]. **siccus**, -a, -um *dry.* **harena** (arena), -ae, f. *sand.* **ignei spiritus:** gen. **torqueo**, -ere, torsi, tortum *twist.* **vibratus**, -a, -um *shaken, agitated.* **discursus**, -us, m. *running to and fro, zigzag, flash of lightning.* **rupta** (< rumpo) with **nubes. dehisco**, -ere *gape, yawn, open.* **fulguribus** "flashes of lightning" [i.e. what we call sheet lightning]; both ablative and dative in a stylistic device called ἀπὸ κοινοῦ (apo koinou). The dative is with **similes**, the ablative (of comparison, "than") with **maiores.**

(10) Tum vero idem ille ex Hispania amicus acrius et instantius "si frater" inquit "tuus, tuus avunculus vivit, vult esse vos salvos; si periit, superstites voluit: proinde quid cessatis evadere?" Respondimus non commissuros nos ut de salute illius incerti nostrae consuleremus.

(11) Non moratus ultra proripit se effusoque cursu periculo aufertur. Nec multo post illa nubes descendere in terras, operire maria; cinxerat Capreas et absconderat; Miseni quod procurrit abstulerat.

(12) Tum mater orare, hortari, iubere quoquo modo fugerem; posse enim iuvenem, se et annis et corpore gravem bene morituram, si mihi causa mortis non fuisset. Ego contra salvum me nisi una non futurum; dein manum eius amplexus, addere gradum cogo. Paret aegre incusatque se quod me moretur.

---

10   **instantius** (comp. adv.) *more insistently.* **pereo,** -ire , -ii/ivi, -itum *perish.*
superstes, -stitis (adj.) *surviving, still alive.* **proinde** *therefore, in the same way.*
cesso (1) freq. of **cedo** *hesitate.* **non commissuros nos:** *we would not allow*
ourselves to (+ jussive noun clause with **ut** + subjunctive). **de salute illius**
incerti *uncertain about his safety* [that is, uncle Pliny's the Elder] **nostrae**
saluti dative with **consuleremus** *consider, take thought for.*

11   **moror** (1) *delay.* **effusus** (< **effundo**) *disorderly:* **effuso cursu:** abl. of means/
manner. **periculo:** abl. of separation. **descendere, operire** (*cover*): historical
infinitives (translate as past tense indicatives). **cingo,** -ere, cinxi, cinctum *go*
around, surround. **abscondo,** -ere, -condi, -conditum *put out of sight, hide.*
Miseni ... abstulerat *removed from sight the promontory* (**quod procurrit**) *of*
Misenum.

12   **orare, hortari, iubere:** historical infinitives: translate "began to." **fugerem:**
jussive noun clause after **iubere.** **iuvenem** acc. subject of infinitive: the idea
is "since I was young, I could..." **posse:** infinitive in indirect statement. **se =**
Pliny's mother, Plinia. **morituram** [**esse**]: future infinitive of *morior, mori/
moriri, mortuus/a sum (fut. participle **moriturus**). **una** (adv.) *together with*
(her). **futurum** [**esse**] indirect statement. **dein = deinde** *next.* **amplector,** -i,
amplectus/a sum *embrace, grasp.* **addere gradum** *to quicken* [her] *pace, pick*
up her step. **pareo,** -ere, parui *obey, comply.* **aegre** *with difficulty, reluctantly.*
incuso (1) *accuse, blame.* **quod** with subjunctive, of a cause not the writer's
own. **moror** (1) delay.

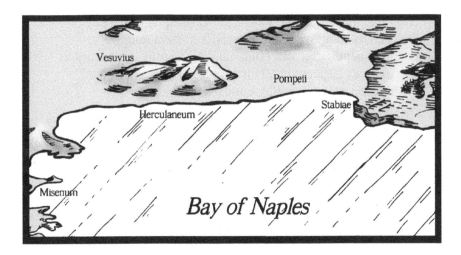

Bay of Naples

(13) Iam cinis, adhuc tamen rarus: respicio; densa caligo tergis imminebat, quae nos torrentis modo infusa terrae sequebatur. "Deflectamus" inquam, "dum videmus ne in via strati comitantium turba in tenebris obteramur."

(14) Vix consideramus, et nox, non qualis inlunis aut nubila, sed qualis in locis clausis lumine extincto. Audires ululatus feminarum, infantum quiritatus, clamores virorum: alii parentes, alii liberos, alii coniuges vocibus requirebant, vocibus noscitabant: hi suum casum, illi suorum miserabantur: erant qui metu mortis mortem precarentur:

---

13 **cinis**, -eris, m. *ashes*. **caligo**, -inis f. *mist, fog, darkness*. **tergum**, -i, n. *back*. **quae ... sequebatur** "which, spread over the land like (in the manner of) a torrent, was following us." **deflecto**, -ere, -flexi, flectum *turn aside*. **sterno**, -ere, stravi, stratum *spread, throw to the ground*. **comitantium turba** *the mob of those following*. **tenebrae**, -arum, f.pl. *darkness*. **obtero**, -ere -trivi, -tritum *trample, flatten*.

14 **consido**, -ere *sit down, settle*. **inlunis**, -e *moonless*. **nubilus**, -a, -um *cloudy, overcast*. **qualis**, -e *such as, like*. **audires**: potential subjunctive, "you would have heard." **ululatus**, -us, m. *wailing*. **quiritatus** *wailing, whining*. **vocibus noscitabant** "they were trying to recognize them by their voices." **miseror** (1) *pity, feel sorry for*. **metu**: abl. of cause. **precor** (1) *pray for*.

(15) multi ad deos manus tollere, plures nusquam iam deos illos, aeternamque illam et novissimam noctem mundo interpretabantur. Nec defuerunt qui fictis mentitisque terroribus vera pericula augerent. Aderant qui Miseni illud ruisse, illud ardere, falso sed credentibus, nuntiabant.

(16) Paulum reluxit; quod non dies nobis sed adventantis ignis indicium videbatur. Et ignis quidem longius substitit, tenebrae rursus, cinis rursus multus et gravis. Hunc identidem adsurgentes excutiebamus: operti alioqui atque etiam oblisi pondere essemus.

(17) Possem gloriari non gemitum mihi, non vocem parum fortem in tantis periculis excidisse, nisi me cum omnibus, omnia mecum perire misero, magno tamen mortalitatis solacio credidissem.

(18) Tandem illa caligo tenuata quasi in fumum nebulamve discessit: mox dies verus, sol etiam effulsit, luridus tamen, qualis esse, cum deficit, solet. Occursabant trepidantibus adhuc oculis mutata omnia altoque cinere, tamquam nive, obducta.

---

15 **nusquam** (adv.) *nowhere.* **mundus**, -i, m. *world.* **interpretor** (1) *explain, understand.* **fingo**, -ere *fabricate.* **mentior**, -iri, mentitus/a sum *lie.* **ruo**, -ere, rui *fall to ruins.* **ardeo**, -ere, -si, -sum *be on fire.* **falso sed credentibus** "falsely but to people who believed them."

16 **paulum** (adv.) *a little.* **reluceo**, -ere, -luxi *shine back/again, shine.* **indicium**, -i, n. *evidence, sign.* **longius substitit** [the fire] *stopped some distance away.* **tenebrae**, -arum, f.pl. *darkness.* **identidem** (adv.) *repeatedly, again and again.* **excutio**, -ere, -cussi, -cussum *shake off.* **operti** < **operio** (see 13). **alioqui** *in some other way, otherwise.* **oblido**, -ere *squeeze together, crush to pieces.*

17 **glorior** (1) *boast.* **gemitus**, -us, m. *groan, sigh.* **mihi**: dat. of separation. **parum** (adv.) *little, not enough.* **misero**, **magno** with **solacio**; **solacium**, -i, n. *comfort, relief.*

18 **tenuo** (1) *make thin, rarefy* [> Engl. *tenuous, attenuate*]. **effulgeo**, -ere, -si *shine out, gleam.* **luridus**, -a, -um *dim, gloomy, murky.* **cum deficit** *when there is an eclipse.* **occurso** (1) *run to meet.* **nix**, nivis, f. *snow.* **obduco** *draw before, cover over, overwhelm.*

(19) Regressi Misenum, curatis utcumque corporibus suspensam dubiamque noctem spe ac metu exegimus. Metus praevalebat: nam et tremor terrae perseverabat et plerique lymphati terrificis vaticinationibus et sua et aliena mala ludificabantur.

(20) Nobis tamen ne tunc quidem, quamquam et expertis periculum et exspectantibus, abeundi consilium, donec de avunculo nuntius. Haec nequaquam historia digna non scripturus leges et tibi, scilicet qui requisisti, inputabis, si digna ne epistula quidem videbuntur. Vale.

---

19 **Misenum** (acc. of place to which: with names of cities and towns the preposition is omitted) *to Misenum.* **utcumque** *whenever, somehow, however it might be, in some way or another.* **suspensus**, -a, -um *suspended, in suspense, anxious, on tenterhooks.* **spe ac metu**: abl. of cause. **exigo**, -ere, -egi, -actum *spend, pass.* **plerique**, -aeque, -aque *very many.* **lymphatus**, -a, -um *crazed, distracted.* **vaticinatio**, -onis, f. *prediction.* **ludificor** (1) *ridicule, mock, turn into a joke.*

20 **experior**, -iri, -pertus/a sum *try, experience.* **abeundi** < **abeo**, -ire. **nequaquam** (adv.) *not at all, by no means.* **historia, epistula** abl. with **digna** (neut. pl. with **haec**), *worthy of.* **tibi inputabis** *you will lay it to your own account.*

Letter 5: *Epistulae* I.9
Escape from daily life in the city

C. PLINIUS MINICIO FUNDANO SUO S.

(1) Mirum est quam singulis diebus in urbe ratio aut constet aut constare videatur, pluribus iunctisque non constet.

(2) Nam si quem interroges "hodie quid egisti?", respondeat "officio togae virilis interfui, sponsalia aut nuptias frequentavi, ille me ad signandum testamentum, ille in advocationem, ille in consilium rogavit."

(3) Haec quo die feceris necessaria, eadem, si cotidie fecisse te reputes, inania videntur, multo magis cum secesseris. Tunc enim subit recordatio "quot dies quam frigidis rebus absumpsi."

Date: before Pliny's appointment to prefecture of Saturn.

Minicius Fundanus: addressed in several letters, he appears to have been consul and then proconsul in Asia under Hadrian. He was a student of Stoic philosophy.

Review indirect question (A&G 574); future less vivid conditions (A&G 516); time constructions (A&G 423-4); accusative of exclamation (A&G 397 d); ablative of comparison (A&G 406).

1 *singuli, -ae, -a, adj. pl. *one at a time*. *ratio constat *the account balances*. Pliny frequently uses terms from the business world, extended to everyday life.

2 officio *at a ceremony*. toga virilis *the toga of manhood*. This refers to the coming of age ceremony in which Roman boys became men, symbolized by their changing the boy's toga with its broad purple border for the plain white manly toga. The age varies, but for the most part, it took place between 14 and 16. nuptiae, -arum, f. pl. *marriage*. frequento (1) *visit*. sponsalia, -ium, n.pl. *betrothal*. signo (1) *set a mark on, seal*. in advocationem *into consultation*.

3 reputo (1) *count over, think back*. *inanis, -e *vain, empty* [> Engl. *inane, inanition*]. cum secesseris *when you have gone on vacation* (cf. III.5. 14 in secessu *on vacation*.]. subeo, -ire, -ii/ivi, -itum *go down, come over*. recordatio, -onis, f. *calling to mind, recollection*. *quot (indecl. adj.) *how many*. *absumo, -ere, sumpsi, sumptum *use, spend, waste*.

(4) Quod evenit mihi, postquam in Laurentino meo aut lego aliquid aut scribo aut etiam corpori vaco, cuius fulturis animus sustinetur.

(5) Nihil audio quod audisse, nihil dico quod dixisse paeniteat: nemo apud me quemquam sinistris sermonibus carpit, neminem ipse reprehendo, nisi tamen me, cum parum commode scribo; nulla spe, nullo timore sollicitor, nullis rumoribus inquietor: mecum tantum et cum libellis loquor.

(6) O rectam sinceramque vitam, o dulce otium honestumque ac paene omni negotio pulchrius. O mare, o litus, verum secretum mouseion, quam multa invenitis, quam multa dictatis.

(7) Proinde tu quoque strepitum istum inanemque discursum et multum ineptos labores, ut primum fuerit occasio, relinque teque studiis vel otio trade.

---

4   **in meo Laurentino** *at my Laurentine villa.* This villa, on the coast, south of Ostia, is described in remarkable detail in II.17. Many attempts have been made to draw its floorplan. Pliny found this setting most productive of literary work. In a bad year at his other estates, he claimed profit from his Laurentine: *Nihil quidem ibi possideo praeter tectum et hortum statimque harenas, solum tamen mihi in reditu. Ibi enim plurimum scribo, nec agrum quem non habeo sed ipsum me studiis excolo; ac iam possum tibi ut aliis in locis horreum* (**horreus** granary, grain silo) *plenum, sic ibi scrinium* (writing desk) *ostendere.* (IV.6.2). **vacare alicui rei** *be free to attend to a thing, have leisure time for something.* **fultura,**-ae,f. *prop, stay, support.*

5   *paenitet, -ere, -uit *it causes regret* + gen. (of the thing that causes regret) and acc. (of the person who feels regret). **carpo** *pick, pluck, slander, calumniate.* **sinister,** -tra, -trum *left, wrong, perverse* [> Engl. *ambisinistrous*]. **sollicito** (1) *disturb, worry, bother.* **inquieto** (1) *disturb a person's peace of mind.* *tantum (adv.) *only.*

6   **secretus,** -a, -um *separate, remote, private.* **mouseion** (< Greek; cf. Engl. *museum*) *shrine of the Muses.* Many wealthy Romans of literary ambitions justified their affluence by using their villas as places to devote themselves to writing.

7   *proinde *therefore, in the same way.* **strepitus,** -us, m. *noise.* **discursus,**-us, m. *a running about.* *multum: (adv.) *much, very.* *ut primum *as soon as.* *trado, -ere, tradidi, traditum *give/hand over, surrrender.*

(8) Satius est enim, ut Atilius noster eruditissime simul et facetissime dixit, otiosum esse quam nihil agere. Vale.

8   **Atilius noster**: Atilius Crescens from Milan (about 30 miles from Comum), a close friend of Pliny, was a man of meager circumstances, known for his wit and his devotion to learning (quoted again in II.14.2). Letter VI.8 is about their friendship which Pliny describes in the warmest terms, even making himself Achilles to Atilius' Patroclus. *simul (adv.) *at the same time.* **facetus**, -a, -um *fine, elegant, witty.* **otiosus**, -a, -um *at leisure.* To Romans, leisure (**otium**) was the positive of which **negotium** (*business* or *lack of leisure*) was the negative. The English *otiose* which has come to mean *lazy, ineffective, indolent* does not carry the positive Roman connotation.

Letter 6: Episulae I. 5
The informer Regulus

C. PLINIUS VOCONIO ROMANO SUO S.

(1) Vidistine quemquam M. Regulo timidiorem humiliorem post Domitiani mortem? sub quo non minora flagitia commiserat quam sub Nerone, sed tectiora. Coepit vereri ne sibi irascerer; nec fallebatur, irascebar.

Date: the first month of 97, from the reference to the ceremony of the Praetors' new year in section 11.

Voconius Rufus: a literary equestrian, friend of Pliny from Saguntum in Spain, now resident in Italy, for whom Pliny secured senatorial status and other favors from Nerva and Trajan. Seven letters are addressed to him.

Review: subjunctive with verbs of fearing (dependent subjunctive Appendix C; A&G 564); indirect statement (A&G 577-84); future passive periphrastic (A&G 193-4); gerunds (A&G 501-7); genitive with verbs of remembering and forgetting (A&G 350); ablative of comparison (a category of ablative of separation Appendix A; A&G 406)

1   **M. Aquilius Regulus**, an infamous *delator* (informer) under Nero. Although mocked by Pliny and others of his circle as a bad man and a banal orator, he won many prosecutions for *maiestas* (treason: the whole expression is *maiestas minuta*; cf. *lèse majesté*; Engl. *lese majesty*), including those of three consulars, and became very rich from the reward money granted by the emperor. He is one of the few acquaintances that Pliny detests. See also Tacitus, *Histories* 4.42. After the end of Nero's regime, Regulus gave up openly informing, but even so he barely escaped condemnation under Nerva. Other letters referring to him are II. 20; IV.7; VI.2 in which Pliny misses him after his death. **post Domitiani mortem**: Domitian, who had been Regulus' patron, was assassinated on Sept. 18, 96 C.E. The very next day the Senate accepted Nerva as emperor. Soon afterwards the Senate began actions against the minor figures of Domitian's Reign of Terror, those below senatorial rank. Pliny is considering taking action against a more important figure. **tectiora** comparative of tectus *hidden, concealed, covert,* perf. pass. participle of **tego** *to cover.* Silver Age writers make frequent use of comparatives of verbal adjectives. *irascor, -i, iratus/a sum *be angry.* *fallo, -ere, fefelli, falsum *deceive;* pass. *be mistaken.*

(2) Rustici Aruleni periculum foverat, exsultaverat morte, adeo ut librum recitaret publicaretque, in quo Rusticum insectatur atque etiam Stoicorum simiam appellat; adicit Vitelliana cicatrice stigmosum.

(3) Agnoscis eloquentiam Reguli. Lacerat Herennium Senecionem, tam intemperanter quidem ut dixerit ei Mettius Carus, "quid tibi cum meis mortuis? numquid ego Crasso aut Camerino molestus sum?"

(4) quos ille sub Nerone accusaverat. Haec me Regulus dolenter tulisse credebat, ideoque etiam cum recitaret librum, non adhibuerat. Praeterea reminiscebatur quam capitaliter ipsum me apud centumviros lacessisset.

2   **L. Junius Arulenus Rusticus**, a Stoic with an interest in political philosophy; he was executed for treason with the younger Helvidius and Senecio. **periculum,** -i, m. *danger; prosecution.* **foveo,** -ere, fovi *foster, promote.* **exsulto** (1) *exult in, run riot.* *****adeo ut** *to such an extent that* + result clause. **insector** (1, freq. of **insequor**) *pursue, censure, attack.* **simia,** -ae, f. *ape.* **Vitelliana cicatrice stigmosum** *branded by a Vitellian scar,* from a wound received in service to Vitellius, one of the emperors of 69 c.e., succeeded by Vespasian. According to Tacitus (*Histories* 3.80) after the defeat of Vitellius, Rusticus was a peace ambassador to Vespasian. He continued to criticize the Flavians and was condemned.

3   **agnosco,** -ere, -novi, -nitum *recognize, be aware of.* **lacero** (1) *slander, defame, tear to pieces.* **Herennius Senecio,** a friend of Pliny, put to death under Domitian, victim of Mettius Carus. **Mettius Carus,** another notorious informer (see Juvenal 1.36; Tacitus, *Agr.* 45, and Pliny 7.19). He even tried to get Pliny condemned. **"quid tibi cum meis mortuis?"** *"what do* you *have to do with my dead* (i.e. *victims* of my prosecutions)? **molestus,** -a, -um *annoying, harmful;* **molestus/a sum** *interfere with.* **M. Licinius Crassus** was put to death under Nero, a victim of Regulus. **Sulpicius Camerinus,** another victim of Regulus, was accused under Nero, but acquitted.

4   **dolenter fero** *bear with sorrow, take* [it] *hard.* **cum recitaret librum:** Pliny admits that he did not avoid Regulus socially. This refers to a private reading of a new book. Pliny also worked on cases with Regulus after Nero's regime. **adhibeo,** -ere, -hibui, -hibitum *summon, invite.* **reminiscor,** -i *remember.* **capitaliter** (adv.) *lethally, in deadly earnest.* **centumviri:** the Centumviral court, a court which in Pliny's time dealt mainly with cases of inheritance. **lacesso** *challenge, attack.*

(5) Aderam Arrionillae, Timonis uxori, rogatu Aruleni Rustici; Regulus contra. Nitebamur nos in parte causae sententia Meti Modesti, optimi viri: is tunc in exilio erat, a Domitiano relegatus. Ecce tibi Regulus, "quaero" inquit "Secunde, quid de Modesto sentias." Vides quod periculum, si respondissem "bene," quod flagitium, si "male." Non possum dicere aliud tunc mihi quam deos adfuisse. "Respondebo" inquam "si de hoc centumviri iudicaturi sunt." Rursus ille "quaero quid de Modesto sentias."

(6) Iterum ego "solebant testes in reos, non in damnatos interrogari." Tertio ille "non iam quid de Modesto, sed quid de pietate Modesti sentias."

(7) "Quaeris" inquam "quid sentiam; at ego ne interrogare quidem fas puto de quo pronuntiatum est." Conticuit: me laus et gratulatio secuta est, quod nec famam meam aliquo responso, utili fortasse, inhonesto tamen, laeseram nec me laqueis tam insidiosae interrogationis involveram.

(8) Nunc ergo conscientia exterritus adprehendit Caecilianum Celerem, mox Fabium Iustum, rogat ut me sibi reconcilient.

---

5   **aderam** < adsum, -esse, -fui *be present, support* (+ dat.). **Arrionilla**, probably a relative of Arria, wife of Thrasea Paetus (see letter VII.19). **Timon**, very likely one of the philosophers in Rusticus Arulenus' circle. **nitor**, -i, -sus/ xus/a sum *rest, rely on.* **relegatus**, -a, -um *banished, exiled* (a lesser form of banishment than exile, since it did not involve loss of property or civil rights.) **ecce** (interjection) *here's!* It has the effect of presenting the subject directly and dramatically to the reader. *inquam, inquit (defective verb) *I say/said, he says/said.* **flagitium**, -i, n. *disgrace, crime.*

6   *iterum (adv.) *again.* **in reos, non in damnatos: in** *in reference to, about, regarding;* **reus**, -i, m. *accused, defendant.* **pietas**, -tatis, f. *devotion, loyalty.*

7   *fas [est] *it is right.* **pronuntio** (1) *declare publicly.* **conticeo**, -ere, -ticui *fall silent.* **laedo**, -ere, -si, -sum *hurt, wound.* **laqueus**, -i, m. *snare, noose, trap.*

8   **conscientia**, -ae, f. *guilty fear.* **adprehendo**, -ere, prehendi, prehensum *latch onto, buttonhole.* **Caecilianus Celer**, unknown outside of Pliny's letters, possibly the friend who was sent *Ep.* VII.17 on literary recitations. **Fabius Justus:** Tacitus dedicates his *Dialogus* to him, indicating that he was an orator or rhetorical theorist. Sherwin-White suggests that Celer and Justus were friends of the elder Pliny from his work in Spain.

Nec contentus, pervenit ad Spurinnam: huic suppliciter, ut est cum timet abiectissimus, "rogo" inquit "mane videas Plinium domi, sed plane mane (neque enim diutius ferre sollicitudinem possum), et quoquo modo efficias ne mihi irascatur."

(9) Evigilaveram: nuntius a Spurinna: "venio ad te." "Immo ego ad te." Coimus in porticu Liviae, cum alter ad alterum tenderemus. Exponit Reguli mandata, addit preces suas, ut decebat optimum virum pro dissimillimo, parce.

(10) Cui ego "dispicies ipse quid renuntiandum Regulo putes: te decipi a me non oportet. Exspecto Mauricum" (nondum ab exilio venerat): "ideo nihil alterutram in partem respondere tibi possum, facturus quidquid ille decreverit; illum enim esse huius consilii ducem, me comitem decet."

(11) Paucos post dies ipse me Regulus convenit in praetoris officio: illuc persecutus secretum petit: ait timere se ne animo meo penitus haereret quod in centumvirali iudicio aliquando dixisset, cum responderet mihi et Satrio Rufo, "Satrius Rufus, cui non est cum Cicerone aemulatio, et qui contentus est eloquentia saeculi nostri."

(12) Respondi nunc me intellegere maligne dictum, quia ipse confiteretur; ceterum potuisse honorificum existimari. "Est enim" inquam "mihi cum Cicerone aemulatio, nec sum contentus

---

Vestricius Spurinna (see also *Ep.* II.7, and III.1 which describes a visit to Spurinna's house) a respected consular who was consul twice more in 98 and 100 C.E. **suppliciter** (adv.) *in the manner of a suppliant.* **abiectissimus, -a, - um** *most downcast.* *****mane** (adv.) *in the morning.* *****domi** (loc.) *at home.* **plane** (adv.) *clearly, quite.* **diutius** compar. of diu.

9   **evigilo** (1) *be awake* *****immo** (adv.) used in contradiction: *no indeed; yes…but.* **coimus** < **coeo,** -ire, -ii/ivi, -itum *come together, meet.* **tendo,** -ere, -tendi, tentum/tensum *head for.* **parce** (adv.) *sparingly.*

10 **dispicio,** -ere *see through, perceive.* **Junius Mauricus,** brother of Rusticus Arulenus (see Tacitus *Hist.* 4.40; Plutarch, *Galba* 8; Martial 5.28.). **nondum** (adv.) *not yet.* **ideo** *for that reason, therefore.* **alteruter** *one or the other, either.* **decerno,** -ere, -crevi, -cretum *decide.* **comes,** -itis, m/f. *companion, associate.*

11 **praetoris officio** *in attendance at the installation of the praetor* (on Jan. 1). **secretum, -i,** n. *secret, privacy;* **secretum petere** *ask for a private audience.* **penitus** (adv.) *inwardly, deeply.* **Satrius Rufus,** a senator who at times acted with Pliny (see *Ep.* ix.13.17). **aemulatio,** -onis, f. *rivalry.* **saeculum,** -i, n. *age* [> Engl. *secularism*].

12 **maligne** (adv.) *spitefully, in a derogatory way.* **ceterum** *the rest, otherwise.*

eloquentia saeculi nostri.

(13) Nam stultissimum credo ad imitandum non optima quaeque proponere. Sed tu, qui huius iudicii meministi, cur illius oblitus es in quo me interrogasti quid de Meti Modesti pietate sentirem?" Expalluit notabiliter, quamvis palleat semper, et haesitabundus "interrogavi, non ut tibi nocerem, sed ut Modesto." Vide hominis crudelitatem, qui non dissimulet exuli nocere voluisse.

(14) Subiunxit egregiam causam: "scripsit" inquit "in epistula quadam, quae apud Domitianum recitata est, Regulus, omnium bipedum nequissimus"; quod quidem Modestus verissime scripserat.

(15) Hic fere nobis sermonis terminus. Neque enim volui progredi longius, ut mihi omnia libera servarem, dum Mauricus venit. Nec me praeterit esse Regulum δυσκαθαίρετον: est enim locuples factiosus, curatur a multis, timetur a pluribus, quod plerumque fortius amore est. Potest tamen fieri ut haec concussa labantur.

(16) Nam gratia malorum tam infida est quam ipsi. Verum, ut idem saepius dicam, exspecto Mauricum. Vir est gravis, prudens, multis experimentis eruditus, et qui futura possit ex praeteritis providere. Mihi et temptandi aliquid et quiescendi illo auctore ratio constabit.

(17) Haec tibi scripsi, quia aecum erat te pro amore mutuo non solum omnia mea facta dictaque verum etiam consilia cognoscere. Vale.

---

13 *memini, -isse + gen. obliviscor, -i, oblitus/a sum *forget* + gen. palleo, -ere, -ui *be pale, blanch.* haesitabundus, -a, -um *stammering.* * dissimulo (1) *to pretend that a thing is not what it is.*

14 egregius, -a, -um *extraordinary* [< e + grex, greg- *flock, herd* > Engl. *egregious* which now means "conspicuously bad"]. *nequam (indecl. adj. with compar. nequior, -ius; superl. nequissimus, -a, -um) *worthless, good for nothing.*

15 *plerumque *for the most part, mostly, very often.* *fere (adv.) *almost.* praetereo, -ire, -ii/ivi, -itum *go by, pass, escape one's notice.* δυσκαθαίρετον (dyskathaireton, Greek) *hard to overthrow.* locuples, -etis (adj.) *rich* (< locus + root PLE- *full* as in plenus). factiosus, -a, -um *influential, having a strong factio* (company of partisans, political following). concutio, -ire, -cussi, -cussum *strike together, shake to its foundations, shatter.*

16 gratia, -ae, f. *favor, popularity.* ratio constabit *the account will balance.*

17 aecum = aequum.

Letter 7: Pliny *Epistulae* VII.19
Illness of Fannia

C. Plinius Prisco Suo S.

(1) Angit me Fanniae valetudo. Contraxit hanc dum assidet Iuniae virgini, sponte primum –est enim affinis– deinde etiam ex auctoritate pontificum.

(2) Nam virgines, cum vi morbi atrio Vestae coguntur excedere, matronarum curae custodiaeque mandantur. Quo munere Fannia dum sedulo fungitur, hoc discrimine implicita est.

Priscus: this particular *Priscus* is not identified with certainty; possibly Cornelius Priscus to whom III.21 is also addressed.

Fannia, the remarkable granddaughter of another admirable woman, Arria the Elder, has fallen gravely ill. In this letter Pliny describes the emotions and almost physical distress he feels over the illness of his friend. Fannia was the second wife of Helvidius Priscus with whom she twice went into exile, first under Nero and then under Vespasian. Helvidius was executed ca. 75 C.E., more than thirty years before the date of this letter. Fannia died about 107.

1   **ango**, -ere *draw tight, strangle, torment, trouble*: Pliny uses a verb associated with illness, as if the respiratory infection that has laid Fannia low is causing him a sympathetic constriction of the lungs. **valetudo**, -inis, f. *health*, often *ill health*. **contraho**, -ere, -traxi, -tractum *draw together, contract* (of a disease). **assideo**, -ere, -edi *sit by, attend* (in illness) + dative. **virgini**: that is, **Vestali**. (See Aulus Gellius I.12 on Vestals.) **sponte** (adv.) *of one's own free will, voluntarily*. **affinis**, -is, m/f. *relation by marriage*. **deinde** (adv.) *then, later*. **pontifex**, -icis, m. *priest*. The College of Pontiffs were in charge of the Vestals.

2   **morbus**, -i, m. *illness*. **atrio Vestae**: *Atrium Vestae*, a compound east of the Forum Romanum that included the temple and grove of Vesta as well as the Vestals' house. **excedo**, -ere, -cessi, -cessum *go out, leave*. **matrona**, -ae, f. *married woman*. **mando** (1) *entrust*. **munus**, -eris, n. *gift, duty*. **sedulo** (adv.) *diligently*. **fungor**, -i, functus/a sum *perform* + ablative. **discrimen**, -inis, n. *division, distinction, crisis, danger*. The term is used in judicial settings, and perhaps Pliny uses it here in anticipation of the next sections in which he writes about Fannia's trials and perils in court. **implico** (1) *entangle, be made sick*.

(3) Insident febres, tussis increscit; summa macies summa defectio. Animus tantum et spiritus viget Helvidio marito, Thrasea patre dignissimus; reliqua labuntur, meque non metu tantum, verum etiam dolore conficiunt.

(4) Doleo enim feminam maximam eripi oculis civitatis, nescio an aliquid simile visuris. Quae castitas illi, quae sanctitas, quanta gravitas quanta constantia! Bis maritum secuta in exsilium est, tertio ipsa propter maritum relegata.

(5) Nam cum Senecio reus esset quod de vita Helvidi libros composuisset rogatumque se a Fannia in defensione dixisset, quaerente minaciter Mettio Caro, an rogasset respondit: "Rogavi";

---

3   **insideo**, -ere, -sedi *settle upon, take over.* Through his use of compounds from the root sed-, Pliny shows how Fannia contracted her illness (**assidet** 1, **sedulo** 2) and how it progressed (**insident**, 3). He is almost clinical in his observation of the disease. **febris**, -s, f. *fever.* **tussis**, -is, f. *cough.* **macies**, –, f. *thinness, wasting away.* **defectio**, -onis, f. *loss of strength.* **vigeo**, -ere, -ui *thrive, be lively.* **Helvidio marito, Thrasea patre**: ablatives with dignissimus ("of"). P. Fannius Thrasea Paetus was, for his outspokenness, forced to commit suicide under Nero (66 C.E.). This would be thought great praise for a woman, that she is worthy of her father and husband. **reliqua**: neuter pl., subject of **labuntur**, "everything else," "all the rest." **labor**, -i, lapsus/a sum *slip, slide.* **non ... tantum, verum etiam** *not only, but also.* **metus**, -us, m. *fear.* **dolor**, -oris, m. *sadness, grief.* **conficio**, -ere, -feci, -fectum *perform, consume, overwhelm.*

4   **doleo**, -ere, -ui (doliturus) *feel pain, grieve.* **eripio**, -ere, -ui, -reptum *snatch away.* **visuris**: with **oculis**. **castitas**, -tatis, f. *purity.* **sanctitas**, -tatis, f. *sacredness, integrity.* **gravitas**, -tatis, f. *weight, dignity, presence*: THE Roman virtue, now in common use as a desirable quality for presidents. **constantia**, -ae, f. *steadiness, consistency, self-possession.* **bis** (adv.) *twice.* In 66 C.E. Helvidius was first exiled for his relation to Thrasea (see 3, above); he returned after the death of Nero. He opposed Vespasian's policies and was exiled again, around 75 C.E. **maritus**, -i, m. *husband.* **tertio** (adv. < **tertius**) *a third time.* **relego** (1) *banish.* This refers to *relegatio*, a milder form of exile without loss of civil rights.

5   **Senecio**, -onis, m. *Herennius Senecio*, another victim of Mettius Carus, was put to death by Domitian for writing this biography of Helvidius Priscus. **reus**, -i, m. *defendant, accused*; as adj. *under charges.* **defensio**, -onis, f. *defense.* **quaerente Mettio Caro**: abl. abs. Mettius Carus was a notorious informer (*delator*) and his name became proverbial; he is mentioned as a bane by Tacitus, Juvenal, and Martial. He even informed against Pliny. See Pliny I.5 on the informer Regulus. **minaciter** (adv.) *threateningly.* **an** *whether* introduces an indirect question following **quaerente**.

an commentarios scripturo dedisset: "Dedi"; an sciente matre: "Nesciente"; postremo nullam vocem cedentem periculo emisit.

(6) Quin etiam illos ipsos libros, quamquam ex necessitate et metu temporum abolitos senatus consulto, publicatis bonis servavit habuit, tulitque in exsilium exsili causam.

(7) Eadem quam iucunda quam comis, quam denique - quod paucis datum est - non minus amabilis quam veneranda! Eritne quam postea uxoribus nostris ostentare possimus? Erit a qua viri quoque fortitudinis exempla sumamus, quam sic cernentes audientesque miremur, ut illas quae leguntur?

(8) Ac mihi domus ipsa nutare, convulsaque sedibus suis ruitura supra videtur, licet adhuc posteros habeat. Quantis enim virtutibus quantisque factis assequentur, ut haec non novissima occiderit?

---

commentarii, -orum, m.pl. *notebooks, documents.* **scripturo** refers to **Senecio**. **matre**: Arria the Younger. **postremo** (adv.) *finally.* **vox**, -cis, f. *utterance.* **cedo**, -ere, -cessi, cessum *yield to.* **emitto**, -ere, -misi, -missum *let out.*

6   **quin etiam** (adv.) *on the contrary.* **quamquam** *although.* **aboleo**, -ere, -evi, -etum *destroy, efface.* **senatus consultum** *a decree of the Senate.* **publicatis bonis** abl. abs. **bona**, -orum, n. pl. *goods, property.* **publico** (1) *confiscate, appropriate to the state.* It was common for the imperial government, always wanting more revenue, to appropriate the property of those sent into exile. **exsilium**, -i, n. *exile.*

7   **iucundus**, -a, -um *pleasant.* **comis**, -e *affable, courteous.* **venerandus**, -a, -um *to be revered, venerable.* **ostento** (1, frequentative of ostendo) *exhibit, hold up* (as an example) *for.* **viri**: subject of **sumamus**. **cerno**, -ere, crevi, cretum *sift, perceive.* **leguntur**: an unusual usage: "are read about." Fannia, like her famous grandmother, has become a legendary feminine icon.

8   **nuto** (1) *nod, sway to and fro*: an apt image since the cosmos shook at Zeus' nod. **convello**, -ere, -velli, -vulsum/volsum *pull off, shake.* **sedes**, -is, f. *seat, foundation.* **ruitura**: future active participle of **ruo**, -ere, -ui, -itus *fall violently, fall down.* **supra** (adv.) *above.* **licet**, -ere, -uit (impersonal) it is permitted; + concessive clause in subjunctive *although.* **posteri**, -orum, m/f. *descendants.* **assequor**, -i, -secutus/a sum *attain* (to + dat.). **novissima**: that is, "the very last (of her family)." **occido**, -ere, -cidi, -casum *fall, sink, go down, set, perish.*

(9) Me quidem illud etiam affligit et torquet, quod matrem eius, illam –nihil possum illustrius dicere –tantae feminae matrem, rursus videor amittere, quam haec, ut reddit ac refert nobis, sic auferet secum, meque et novo pariter et rescisso vulnere afficiet.

(10) Utramque colui utramque dilexi: utram magis nescio, nec discerni volebant. Habuerunt officia mea in secundis, habuerunt in adversis. Ego solacium relegatarum, ego ultor reversarum; non feci tamen paria atque eo magis hanc cupio servari, ut mihi solvendi tempora supersint.

(11) In his eram curis, cum scriberem ad te; quas si deus aliquis in gaudium verterit, de metu non querar. Vale.

9 **affligo**, -ere, -flixi, -flictum *strike down, distress*. **torqueo**, -ere, torsi, tortum *twist, wrench*. Pliny continues the violent physical imagery from the previous section. **illustris**, -e *brilliant, famous, noble*. **rursus** (adv.) *again*. **amitto**, -ere, -misi, missum, *lose*. **quam** refers to Arria. **haec** refers to Fannia. **aufero** -ferre, abstuli, ablatum *take away*. **rescindo**, -ere, -scidi, -scissum *tear open, reopen*. **vulnus**, -eris, n. *wound*. **afficio**, -ere, -feci, -fectum *affect*.

10 **uterque**, utraque, utrumque *each (of two)*. **colo**, -ere, -ui, cultum *cultivate, care for, honor, esteem*. **diligo**, -ere, -lexi, -lectum *value, love*. **uter**, utra, utrum *which (of two)*. **discerno**, -ere, -crevi, -cretum (see **cerno** in 7). *separate, distinguish*. **officium**, -i, n. *duty*. **secundus**, -a, -um *favorable*. **adversus**, -a, -um *adverse, unfavorable*. **solacium**, -i, n. *comfort, relief*. **relegatarum** refers to both Fannia and Arria. On *relegatio*, see 4, above. **ultor**, -oris, m. *avenger*. **paria** n. pl. < **par** *equal*: i.e. equal to what they deserve. It is possible that Pliny feels a twinge of guilt for not having stood up enough for this family. Tacitus (*Agricola* 2. 45) admits that the senate had a hand in imprisoning Helvidius. **solvo**, -ere, solvi, solutum *loosen, pay* (a debt). **supersum**, -esse, -fui *be left*.

11 **eram, scriberem**: epistolary imperfect: when you are writing a letter, you know that by the time your friend receives it, time will have passed so that what is present or future as you write will be past by the time the letter is read. **verterit ... querar**: future perfect and future in a future more vivid condition. **queror**, -i, questus/a sum *complain*.

Letter 8: *Epistulae* IV.13
Pliny helps endow a school in his hometown

C. PLINIUS TACITO SUO S.

(1) Salvum te in urbem venisse gaudeo; venisti autem, si quando alias, nunc maxime mihi desideratus. Ipse pauculis adhuc diebus in Tusculano commorabor, ut opusculum quod est in manibus absolvam.

(2)Vereor enim ne, si hanc intentionem iam in fine intermisero, aegre resumam. Interim ne quid festinationi meae pereat, quod sum praesens petiturus hac quasi praecursoria epistula rogo. Sed prius accipe causas rogandi.

(3) Proxime cum in patria mea fui, venit ad salutandum municipis mei filius praetextatus. Huic ego "studes?" inquam. Respondit

---

Pliny offers matching funds for his compatriots at Comum if they want to establish a school there, and asks his friend Tacitus to recommend teachers.

Review: subjunctive with verbs of fearing (A&G 564); future conditions (A&G 516); gerunds and gerundives (A&G 503-7); ablative absolute (A&G 419); jussive subjunctive (A&G 439, 563).

1   **gaudeo**, -ere, gavisus/a sum (+ indirect statement) *rejoice.* **si quando** *if ever.* **alias** *at another time.* **mihi**: dat. of agent (extended in Silver Latin to use with any compound passive). **pauculis adhuc diebus** *for the next few days.* ***adhuc** (adv.) *still.* **in Tusculano** *at his villa near Tusculum*; cf. **in Laurentino** in I.9. **commoror** (1) *linger, stay on.* **opusculum** *a little work*: a small volume of verses which Pliny refers to also in letter 14 of book IV. ***absolvo**, -ere, -solvi, -solutum *finish off, complete.*

2   ***vereor** -eri, veritus/a *fear* + **ne** (*that, lest*) or **ut** (*that not*) with the subjunctive. **intentio**, -onis, f. *effort.* **intermitto**, -ere, -misi, -missum *interrupt.* ***aegre** (adv.) *with difficulty, reluctantly.* **interim** (adv.) *meanwhile.* **ne quid festinationi meae pereat** *to satisfy my impatience, to waste no time.* **quod**: object of *sum petiturus* (future active periphrastic: *I am going to, I intend*). ***praesens**, -entis *in person.* **hac ... praecursoria epistula** *with this letter as if it is/were a scout.* **quasi** apologizes for the neologism **praecursoria**.

3   **proxime** (adv.) *most recently, last.* **mea patria**, that is, Comum. **ad me salutandum**: the clients came to salute their patrons at dawn. **municeps**, -cipis, m. *fellow citizen, townsman.* **praetextatus** i. e. still wearing the bordered boy's toga, before changing to the **toga virilis** (so under 16 years of age). **Studes**? *do you go to school?*

"etiam." "Ubi?" "Mediolani." "Cur non hic?" Et pater eius (erat enim una atque etiam ipse adduxerat puerum) "quia nullos hic praeceptores habemus."

(4) "Quare nullos? nam vehementer intererat vestra, qui patres estis," et opportune conplures patres audiebant, "liberos vestros hic potissimum discere. Ubi enim aut iucundius morarentur quam in patria aut pudicius continerentur quam sub oculis parentum aut minore sumptu quam domi?

(5) Quantulum est ergo collata pecunia conducere praeceptores, quodque nunc in habitationes, in viatica, in ea quae peregre emuntur (omnia autem peregre emuntur) inpenditis adicere mercedibus? Atque adeo ego, qui nondum liberos habeo, paratus sum pro re publica nostra, quasi pro filia vel parente, tertiam partem eius quod conferre vobis placebit dare.

(6) Totum etiam pollicerer, nisi timerem ne hoc munus meum quandoque ambitu corrumperetur, ut accidere multis in locis video, in quibus praeceptores publice conducuntur.

(7) Huic vitio occurri uno remedio potest, si parentibus solis ius conducendi relinquatur isdemque religio recte iudicandi necessitate collationis addatur.

---

etiam *yes.* **Mediolani** *at Milan* (about 30 miles south of Comum). *__hic__ (adv.) *here.* *__una__ (adv.) *along with, together with* ["the boy" is understood]. *__quia__ (conj.) *because.* **praeceptores** *teachers* (of rhetoric).

4   **vehementer intererat vestra** *it would be ever so much in your interest...* **conplures** *several, quite a few.* *__potissimum__ *most particularly.* **disco**, -ere, didici *learn, be taught.* *__liberi__, -orum, m/f. pl. *children.* **moror** *delay, stay, remain.* **iucundius, pudicius** compar. adverbs, "more —ly" of **iucundus**, **pudicus** *pleasant, modest.* **sumptus**, -us, m. *expense.*

5   **quantulum ... mercedibus** *what a small matter it would be ... to hire teachers ... and what you now spend on ... to add to the salaries.* **habitatio**, -onis, f. *housing, lodging.* **viaticum**, -i, n. *provision for a journey, travel expense.* **peregre** *abroad, away from home.* *__emo__, -ere, emi, emptum *buy.* **inpendo**, -ere *spend.* **nondum** (adv.) *not yet.*

6   **polliceor**, -eri, pollicitus/a sum *promise.* **munus**, -eris, n. *gift.* **quandoque** (adv.) *at some time.* **ambitu corrumperetur** *be perverted to private use*: Pliny fears nepotism in the choice of professors. Intrigue among schoolmasters was regularly expected (Sherwin-White). *__ut__ *as.* **publice** (adv.) *at public expense.*

7   **huic ... potest**: *it is possible for this fault to be met /resisted /obviated.* **religio**, -onis, f. *conscientiousness.* **collatio**, -onis, f. *contribution.*

(8) Nam qui fortasse de alieno neglegentes, certe de suo diligentes erunt dabuntque operam ne a me pecuniam non nisi dignus accipiat, si accepturus et ab ipsis erit.

(9) Proinde consentite, conspirate maioremque animum ex meo sumite, qui cupio esse quam plurimum quod debeam conferre. Nihil honestius praestare liberis vestris, nihil gratius patriae potestis. Educentur hic qui hic nascuntur statimque ab infantia natale solum amare frequentare consuescant. Atque utinam tam claros praeceptores inducatis ut finitimis oppidis studia hinc petantur, utque nunc liberi vestri aliena in loca, ita mox alieni in hunc locum confluant."

(10) Haec putavi altius et quasi a fonte repetenda, quo magis scires quam gratum mihi foret, si susciperes quod iniungo. Iniungo autem et pro rei magnitudine rogo ut ex copia studiosorum, quae ad te ex admiratione ingenii tui convenit, circumspicias praeceptores quos sollicitare possimus, sub ea tamen condicione ne cui fidem meam obstringam. Omnia enim libera parentibus servo. Illi iudicent, illi eligant: ego mihi curam tantum et inpendium vindico.

(11) Proinde si quis fuerit repertus qui ingenio suo fidat, eat illuc ea lege ut hinc nihil aliud certum quam fiduciam suam ferat. Vale. (IV.13)

---

8   *fortasse (adv.) *perhaps.* de alieno *concerning another person's expenditure.* *operam dare *take pains, make an effort.* non nisi dignus *no one who is not worthy, only one who is worthy.*

9   proinde *therefore, so.* conspiro *breathe together: agree, unite* (also, especially in Suetonius, *enter into a conspiracy*). *praesto (1) *offer.* educo (1) *bring up, educate.* *statim (adv.) *immediately.* solum, -i, n. *ground, land, soil.* frequento (1) *visit often, resort to.* utinam *with the subjunctive of wish: would that, if only.* ut (1) *that;* (2) *as.*

10 altius et a fonte *from farther back and from the source.* quo magis scires: relative clause of purpose. iniungo, -ere, -iunxi, -iunctum *enjoin, impose.* pro (conj.) *in proportion to, according to.* sollicito (1) *disturb, harass, invite.* ne cui *after* ne, quis = aliquis. obstringo, -ere, -strinxi, -strinctum *bind, put under an obligation.* eligo, -ere, -legi, -lectum *choose, pick.* *tantum (adv.) *only.* vindico *lay claim to, claim as one's own, arrogate, appropriate.*

11 reperio, -ire, repperi, repertum *find.* fido, -ere, fisus/a sum *trust, have confidence in.* ea lege *on this condition.* fiducia, -ae, f. *assurance, confidence, self-confidence.*

Letter 9A: *Epistulae* VI. 4
Calpurnia recuperates in Campania

C. PLINIUS CALPURNIAE SUAE S.

(1) Numquam sum magis de occupationibus meis questus, quae me non sunt passae aut proficiscentem te valetudinis causa in Campaniam prosequi aut profectam e vestigio subsequi.

(2) Nunc enim praecipue simul esse cupiebam, ut oculis meis crederem quid viribus quid corpusculo apparares, ecquid denique secessus voluptates regionisque abundantiam inoffensa transmitteres.

(3) Equidem etiam fortem te non sine cura desiderarem; est enim suspensum et anxium de eo quem ardentissime diligas interdum nihil scire.

Pliny's wife, **Calpurnia,** is away in Campania—a fabulous vacation spot, frequently used by well-to-do Romans as a healthy place to recover strength during or after an illness—for her health. The likely date is early summer 107 C.E. Pliny is busy in Rome and cannot accompany her. Three letters from this period survive which together form a "valuable document for social history" (Sherwin-White p. 407, ad VII.5) Of this series (VI.4; VI.7; VII.5) he writes further: "They blend together, for the first time in European literature, the role of husband and lover, and like other letters of Pliny cast a favorable light on the attitude of his social equals to marriage."

Review deponents (A&G 190-2; Appendix D).

1 **occupationibus**: either his official functions—Pliny was *curator Tiberis* around this time—but more likely (from the subjects of other letters in this book) his duties as an advocate. **queror, -i, questus/a sum *complain*; with **questus** understand **sum**. **prosequor, -i, -secutus/a sum *escort, accompany*. **e vestigio** (idiom) *immediately, at once*.

2 **praecipue (adv.) *especially*. **simul** (adv.) *together* [with you]. **meis oculis**: dat. with *crederem*; the expression means "see for myself." **apparo** (1) *prepare*; + dat. *add to*. **corpusculum**: diminutive of **corpus**. Here the diminutive is affectionate. **secessus**: genitive. **inoffensus**, -a, -um *without obstruction, without doing harm*. **transmitto**, -ere, -misi, -missum *bear, let pass*.

3 **suspensum et anxium**: the subject is **scire**; the two adjectives have a causative force. **de eo quem**: generic masculine; used here even though the specific cause of his concern is feminine. **interdum (adv.) *sometimes, now and then*.

(4) Nunc vero me cum absentiae tum infirmitatis tuae ratio incerta et varia sollicitudine exterret. Vereor omnia, imaginor omnia, quaeque natura metuentium est, ea maxime mihi quae maxime abominor fingo.

(5) Quo impensius rogo, ut timori meo cottidie singulis vel etiam binis epistulis consulas. Ero enim securior dum lego, statimque timebo cum legero. Vale.

---

4   *cum ... tum *both ... and*. **ratio**, -onis, f. *consideration*. **sollicitudo**, -inis, f. *worry*. *metuo**, -ere, -ui *fear*. **abominor** (1) *deprecate, wish away* [a bad omen]. **fingo**, -ere, finxi, fictum *touch, fashion, imagine*.
5   **quo** (adv.) *wherefore, and therefore*. **impensius** (compar. adv.) *more earnestly*. **bini**, -ae, -a *two each*. **consulo**, -ere, -lui, -ltum *consider, have regard for*.

Letter 9B: Epistulae VI. 7
Mutual admiration society

C. Plinius Calpurniae Suae S.

(1) Scribis te absentia mea non mediocriter affici unumque habere solacium, quod pro me libellos meos teneas, saepe etiam in vestigio meo colloces.

(2) Gratum est quod nos requiris, gratum quod his fomentis acquiescis; invicem ego epistulas tuas lectito atque identidem in manus quasi novas sumo.

(3) Sed eo magis ad desiderium tui accendor: nam cuius litterae tantum habent suavitatis, huius sermonibus quantum dulcedinis inest! Tu tamen quam frequentissime scribe, licet hoc ita me delectet ut torqueat. Vale.

Review partitive genitive and objective genitive (A&G 346; 347-8; Appendix A).

1 **mediocriter** (adv.) *moderately, slightly.* ***quod** *the fact that.* **pro** (prep.) *in place of.* **libellus,** -i, m. (diminutive of **liber**) *a little book, a speech.* Pliny rewrote and published many of his speeches, but the only one to survive is the *Panegyricus* in praise of Trajan. In an earlier letter (IV.19) to Calpurnia's aunt, Calpurnia Hispulla, Pliny reveals his pleasure at his wife's interest in his own literary work. She conceals herself in the next room behind a curtain to listen to his recitations, learns his speeches by heart, and sets his verses to music. **teneas, colloces:** dependent clause in indirect statement. **vestigium,** -i, n. *track, footprint; trace of the presence of a person or thing.* **colloco** (1) *lay, place.* Her letters to him unfortunately do not survive, but here he gives us a hint of their contents.

2 **requiro,** -ere, -quisivi, -quisitum *miss.* **fomentum,** -i, n. *a warm application, alleviation.* **acquiesco,** -ere, -evi *become quiet, rest, find pleasure.* **invicem** (adv.) *in turn.* **lectito** (1; freq. of **lego**) *read over and over, read and reread.* **indentidem** *again and again.*

3 **eo magis** *so much the more.* **accendo,** -ere, -cendi, -censum *kindle, set on fire.* **suavitas,** -tatis, f. *sweetness, pleasantness, the quality of pleasing the senses.* **suavitatis:** partitive genitive. **dulcedo,** -inis, f. *sweetness, pleasantness, charm, pleasure attaching to an action.*

Letter 10: *Epistulae* VII. 4
Pliny's poetical history

C. PLINIUS PONTIO SUO S.

(1) Ais legisse te hendecasyllabos meos; requiris etiam quemadmodum coeperim scribere, homo ut tibi videor severus, ut ipse fatear non ineptus.

(2) Numquam a poetice —altius enim repetam— alienus fui; quin etiam quattuordecim natus annos Graecam tragoediam scripsi. 'Qualem?' inquis. Nescio; tragoedia vocabatur.

(3) Mox, cum e militia rediens in Icaria insula ventis detinerer, Latinos elegos in illud ipsum mare ipsamque insulam feci. Expertus sum me aliquando et heroo, hendecasyllabis nunc primum, quorum hic natalis haec causa est. Legebantur

---

Pontius Allifanus: a senator from Campania, one of Pliny's literary acquaintances.

Review indirect statement (A&G 577-584), indirect question (A&G 574), indirect command (jussive noun clause A&G 563).

1   **ais** (defective verb) *you say*. **hendecasyllabos**: *verses in hendecasyllabic meter:* (< Greek, *consisting of eleven syllables*), also called Phalaecean stanza (xx -◡◡ -◡ -◡ -x, in which x = long or short); it is a meter favored by Martial. Pliny uses the term in a more general sense to refer to his short poems in a variety of meters. In IV.14.2 Pliny tells us he writes these verses whenever he can catch a few moments, in his carriage (cf. his uncle's practice III.5.15-16), in the bath, and over dinner: *in vehiculo, in balineo, inter cenam*. He also lists his subjects, which are pretty much the standard repertoire, including some erotic verses (*lascivia rerum*). **quemadmodum** *how*. **ineptus**, -a, -um *absurd, silly*.

2   **poetice**, -es, f. (Greek formation = ποιητική) *the art of poetry*; **poetice**: ablative. **quin etiam** (adv. adding a new point) *yes and even __, and furthermore*.

3   **militia**, -ae, f. *military service*; he was military tribune in Syria around 81 C.E. **Icaria**: an island not far from Samos, where legend has it Icarus fell to earth. The modern harbor is graced by a magnificent sculpture commemorating his descent. **elegi**, -orum, m. pl. *elegiac verses*. **in** + acc. *into, in reference to*. **herous**, -a, -um *belonging to a hero, heroic*; as a noun: *hexameter* (epic) *verse*. **hic natalis haec causa**: he explains how these verses came into existence and the reason for taking up this style.

in Laurentino: *at my Laurentine villa*. **Asinius Gallus** wrote against the

in Laurentino mihi libri Asini Galli de comparatione patris et Ciceronis. Incidit epigramma Ciceronis in Tironem suum.

(4) Dein cum meridie —erat enim aestas— dormiturus me recepissem, nec obreperet somnus, coepi reputare maximos oratores hoc studii genus et in oblectationibus habuisse et in laude posuisse.

(5) Intendi animum contraque opinionem meam post longam desuetudinem perquam exiguo temporis momento id ipsum, quod me ad scribendum sollicitaverat, his versibus exaravi:

(6) Cum libros Galli legerem, quibus ille parenti
     ausus de Cicerone dare est palmamque decusque,
     lascivum inveni lusum Ciceronis et illo
     spectandum ingenio, quo seria condidit et quo
     humanis salibus multo varioque lepore   5
     magnorum ostendit mentes gaudere virorum.
     Nam queritur quod fraude mala frustratus amantem
     paucula cenato sibi debita savia Tiro

Ciceronian style (see the title of Claudius' response: *Ciceronis defensio adversus Asini Galli libros*, mentioned by Suetonius, *Life of Claudius* 41.3). **patris**: the father of Asinius Gallus, that is, Asinius Pollio, an orator and historian, supporter of Antonius, opponent of Cicero. **incido**, -ere, -cidi, -casum *fall, drop, happen*; **incidit** [something] *presents itself*. **Tiro** was Cicero's secretary and freedman, famous also for his shorthand system called Tironian notes. An erotic relationship between them is uncertain.

4 **meridie** (adv.) *at midday*. **me recipio** *retire, withdraw*. **obrepo**, -ere, -si, -tum *steal over*. **hoc studii genus**: Pliny is careful to justify his whimsical side by citing authorities, serious men of the past who indulged in writing light verse.

5 **animum intendo** *direct one's mind/attention*. **desuetudo**, -inis, f. *disuse*. **perquam** (adv.) *exceedingly*. **exiguus**, -a, -um *slight, small, brief*. **sollicito** (1) *disturb, worry, stimulate*. **exaro** (1) *remove, plough, write* (with a stilus on wax).

6 The meter is dactylic hexameter.

   line 3 **lascivus**, -a, -um *playful, naughty, unrestrained* (referring to the eroticism of the verse). **lusus**, -us, m. *sport, light literary work*.

   line 5 **sal**, salis, m/n. *salt, wit*; pl. *jokes, witticisms*. **lepos**, -oris, m. *charm, wit, pleasantness*.

   line 8 **cenato** < **ceno** (1) *dine*. **savium**, -i, n. *kiss*.

   line 10 **celo** (1) *hide* (> Engl. *conceal*; from the same root: *cell, cellar, occult,*

tempore nocturno subtraxerit. His ego lectis
'cur post haec' inquam 'nostros celamus amores   10
nullumque in medium timidi damus atque fatemur
Tironisque dolos, Tironis nosse fugaces
blanditias et furta novas addentia flammas?'

(7) Transii ad elegos; hos quoque non minus celeriter explicui,
addidi alios facilitate corruptus. Deinde in urbem reversus
sodalibus legi; probaverunt.

(8) Inde plura metra si quid otii, ac maxime in itinere temptavi.
Postremo placuit exemplo multorum unum separatim
hendecasyllaborum volumen absolvere, nec paenitet.

(9) Legitur describitur cantatur etiam, et a Graecis quoque,
quos Latine huius libelli amor docuit, nunc cithara nunc lyra
personatur.

(10) Sed quid ego tam gloriose? Quamquam poetis furere
concessum est. Et tamen non de meo sed de aliorum iudicio
loquor; qui sive iudicant sive errant, me delectat. Unum precor, ut
posteri quoque aut errent similiter aut iudicent. Vale.

clandestine).
7   **sodalis,** -is, m. *member of an association, intimate companion.*
8   **separatim** (adv.) *apart from the others, separately.* This may well be the
    opusculum Pliny refers to in IV.13 that he is finishing up at his Tusculan estate,
    after his trip to Comum.
9   **describitur:** *copies are being made.* **cantatur:** see Pliny's letter to his wife's aunt
    (in which he writes: IV.19.4 *Versus quidem meos cantat etiam formatque* [sets
    to music] *cithara non artifice* [artist] *aliquo docente, sed amore qui magister est
    optimus.*) **Latine** (adv.) *in Latin.* **cithara,** -ae, f. *cithara* [> Engl. *guitar*], *lyre.*
    lyra, -ae, f. *lyre.* The cithara was the instrument for public concerts; the lyre
    was used for more intimate soirees (Sherwin-White p. 406; *ad loc.*). **persono**
    (1) *make noise, resound, sing, chant.*
10 **gloriose** (adv.) *boastingly.* **furo,** -ere *be out of one's mind.* **iudico** (1) *judge,
    exercise* [good] *judgment.*

Letter 11: *Epistulae* X. 90
Water supply for Sinope

C. PLINIUS TRAIANO IMPERATORI

(1) Sinopenses, domine, aqua deficiuntur; quae videtur et bona et copiosa ab sexto decimo miliario posse perduci. Est tamen statim ab capite paulo amplius passus mille locus suspectus et mollis, quem ego interim explorari modico impendio iussi, an recipere et sustinere opus possit.

(2) Pecunia curantibus nobis contracta non deerit, si tu, domine, hoc genus operis et salubritati et amoenitati valde sitientis coloniae indulseris.

Some of the most interesting letters written by Pliny to Trajan during his stint in Bithynia concern public works and engineering projects (e.g. X.17; 23; 37; 39; 41; 49; 61; 70; 81; 98). This letter was written during Pliny's second year in the province.

1   **Sinopenses** m/f. pl. *citizens of Sinope*, a major port city in Pontus. **domine** in addressing the emperor both equestrian procurators and freedmen used **dominus** (see Sherwin-White ad x.2). **aqua**: abl. with deficiuntur. **miliarium**, -i, n. *milestone*. **caput**, -itis, n. *head, origin, source*. **paulo** (adv.) *a little*. **passus mille** *a mile*; **amplius mille passus** *more than a mile*. **suspectus**, -a, -um *mistrusted, doubtful*. **mollis**, -e *soft, pliant, lacking firmness*. **impendium**, -i, n. *expense*; **impendio modico**: abl. of price.

2   **contractus**, -a, -um *drawn together, collected*. **desum**, -esse, -fui *be lacking*. **salubritas**, -tatis, f. *wholesomeness, good health*. **amoenitas**, -tatis, f. *pleasantness*. **valde** (adv.) *very, intensely*. **sitio**, -ire, -ive *be thirsty*; **sitiens**, -entis *thirsty, dry*. **indulgeo**, -ere, -si *concede, grant*.

Epistulae X. 91
Trajan's Reply

TRAIANUS PLINIO

Ut coepisti, Secunde carissime, explora diligenter, an locus ille quem suspectum habes sustinere opus aquae ductus possit. Neque dubitandum puto, quin aqua perducenda sit in coloniam Sinopensem, si modo et viribus suis assequi potest, cum plurimum ea res et salubritati et voluptati eius collatura sit.

Trajan's answer follows Pliny's wording very closely, without the personal touch found in some of his letters. Throughout the correspondence, the emperor is primarily interested in fiscal responsibility on the part of the provincial cities and towns. As long as the locals can pay for an improvement, if it adds to civic life and does not offer an opportunity for factions or rebellion (as in X.34 where Trajan says no to a fire brigade), it will usually receive imperial approval.

an *whether.* **aquae ductus** *aqueduct.* **viribus suis:** *with its own resources.* **assequor, -i, -secutus/a sum** *follow up, accomplish.* **potest:** the subject is Sinope. **ea res** refers to the project. **eius** refers to Sinope. **collatura < confero.**

Letter 12: *Epistulae* X.120
Pliny's last letter

C. PLINIUS TRAIANO IMPERATORI

(1) Usque in hoc tempus, domine, neque cuiquam diplomata commodavi neque in rem ullam nisi tuam misi. Quam perpetuam servationem meam quaedam necessitas rupit.

(2) Uxori enim meae audita morte avi volenti ad amitam suam excurrere usum eorum negare durum putavi, cum talis officii gratia in celeritate consisteret, sciremque te rationem itineris probaturum, cuius causa erat pietas. Haec tibi scripsi, quia mihi parum gratus fore videbar, si dissimulassem inter alia beneficia hoc unum quoque me debere indulgentiae tuae, quod fiducia eius quasi consulto te non dubitavi facere, quem si consuluissem, sero fecissem.

Pliny was very scrupulous in his use of the imperial post (see X.45). Thanks to his care we have this last letter written after he has sent his wife on her mission of family piety. It is likely that he died some time during this year. What happened to Calpurnia is anybody's guess.

1   ***usque** *up to now*. **diplomata** *documents, permits* to use the imperial courier service. **commodo** (1) *give, lend, oblige*. **servatio,** -onis, f. *maintenance, observance* (of a practice).

2   **uxori** = Calpurniae (see letters VI.4 and 7 in this collection; also VII.5; VII.10-11, and IV.19).

     amita, -ae, f. *aunt*: Calpurnia Hispulla (see letters IV.19 and VII.11). **gratia,** -ae, f. *favor, service, courtesy*. **consisto,** -ere, -stiti *stand, depend on*. **pietas,** -tatis, f. *family duty*. **dissimulo** (1) *pretend*. **fiducia,** -ae, f. *confidence, trust, security*. **eius** refers to **indulgentia**. **sero** (adv.) *late, too late*.

Epistulae X.121
Trajan's reply

TRAIANUS PLINIO

Merito habuisti, Secunde carissime, fiduciam animi mei nec
dubitandum fuisset, si exspectasses donec me consuleres, an iter
uxoris tuae diplomatibus, quae officio tuo dedi, adiuvandum
esset, cum apud amitam suam uxor tua deberet etiam celeritate
gratiam adventus sui augere.

---

merito (adv.) *deservedly, justly, according to* (one's) *desert.*

Some Letters of Pliny for Reading at Sight

Epistulae I.11

C. PLINIUS FABIO IUSTO SUO S.

Olim mihi nullas epistulas mittis. Nihil est, inquis, quod scribam. At hoc ipsum scribe nihil esse quod scribas, vel solum illud unde incipere priores solebant "si vales, bene est; ego valeo." Hoc mihi sufficit; est enim maximum. Ludere me putas? serio peto. Fac sciam quid agas, quod sine sollicitudine summa nescire non possum. Vale.

Pliny writes to his friend Fabius Justus (a fellow advocate and senator) to point out that he has not heard from him for a long time. This letter is formulaic in its entirety, like a postcard, and though short on content it offers some useful idioms. Such letters crop up throughout the collection.

olim = iamdudum *now for a long time* [a late usage]. **quod scribam**: relative clause of characteristic. **unde** *whence, with which.* **si vales, bene est, ego valeo** (often abbreviated S.V.B.E.E.V.) **priores** *ancestors, old-timers.* **sufficio** *meet the need, be enough for.* **ludo** *play, mock, kid.* **serio** *seriously, in earnest.* **fac sciam** substantive clause of result ("let me know") **sollicitudo,** -tudinis, f. *worry, concern*

Epistulae X. 88-89

C. PLINIUS TRAIANO IMPERATORI

Opto, domine, et hunc natalem et plurimos alios quam
felicissimos agas aeternaque laude florentem virtutis tuae gloriam
incolumis et fortis aliis super alia operibus augeas.

TRAIANUS PLINIO S.

Agnosco vota tua, mi Secunde carissime, quibus precaris ut
plurimos et felicissimos natales florente statu rei publicae nostrae
agam.

Epistulae VII.5

C. PLINIUS CALPURNIAE SUAE S.

Incredibile est quanto desiderio tui tenear. In causa amor
primum, deinde quod non consuevimus abesse. Inde est quod
magnam noctium partem in imagine tua vigil exigo, inde quod
interdiu quibus horis te visere solebam ad diaetam tuam ipsi me,
ut verissime dicitur, pedes ducunt, quod denique aeger et maestus
ac similis excluso a vacuo limine recedo. Unum tempus his
tormentis caret, quo in foro amicorum litibus conteror. Aestima
tu quae vita mea sit, cui requies in labore, in miseria curisque
solacium. Vale. (VII. 5)

---

(88) Happy Birthday, Emperor and (89) thank you, my dear fellow.

ago, -ere, egi, actum *pass, spend* [time]. **agas, augeas** subjunctives with **opto** [ut].
incolumis, -e *intact, unharmed; undamaged in health, position, power.* **agnosco**,
-ere, -novi, -nitum *recognize, acknowledge.*

Pliny misses his wife.

primum (adv.). **deinde** (adv.) *then, next.* **consuesco**, -ere, consuevi *become
accustomed.* **abesse** < absum. **inde est quod** *it is for this reason that.* **vigil** (adj.)
awake. **exigo** *spend, pass.* **interdiu** (adv.) *during the day.* **diaeta** *apartment.* **pedes**
< pes, pedis. **denique** *finally.* **aeger** *ill, sorrowful, weak.* **maestus** *sad, sorrowful.*
limen, -inis n. *doorway.* **careo** -ere *be free from* [+ abl.]. **lis**, litis f. *quarrel, dispute,
lawsuit.* **conteror** *I am being worn out.* **aestimo** -are *think* (hint: **aestima** is
imperative). **solacium** *comfort.*

Epistulae I.24

C.PLINIUS BAEBIO HISPANO SUO S.

(1) Tranquillus, contubernalis meus, vult emere agellum quem venditare amicus tuus dicitur. Rogo cures quanti aecum est emat: ita enim delectabit emisse.

(2) Nam mala emptio semper ingrata, eo maxime, quod exprobare stultitiam domino videtur.

(3) In hoc autem agello, si modo adriserit pretium, Tranquilli mei stomachum multa sollicitant, vicinitas urbis, opportunitas viae, mediocritas villae, modus ruris, qui avocet magis quam distringat.

(4) Scholasticis porro dominis, ut hic est, sufficit abunde tantum soli ut relevare caput, reficere oculos, reptare per limitem unamque semitam terere omnisque viticulas suas nosse et numerare arbusculas possint.

(5) Haec tibi exposui, quo magis scires quantum esset ille mihi, ego tibi debiturus, si praediolum istud, quod commendatur his dotibus, tam salubriter emerit ut paenitentiae locum non relinquat. Vale.

---

1 **Tranquillus** = Suetonius, the famous archivist and biographer, is looking for a small farm to buy. Pliny writes to an acquaintance, Baebius Hispanus, who has a friend who is trying to sell a piece of real estate. Pliny tries to get a good deal for Suetonius in part by stressing the small size of the property through the use of diminutives. **contubernalis** *comrade, buddy.* **agellus** = *a small ager.* **vendito** *try to sell, hawk.* **quanti**: gen. of price: *for as much as.* **aecum** = **aequum** *fair.* **eo ... quod** *for the reason that.*

2 **emptio**, -onis, f. *purchase* (cf. buyer's regret). **exprobo** *make a matter of reproach, accuse of, charge with.*

3 **stomachus** lit. *gullet;* > *taste, liking, good-humor;* also *distaste.* **sollicito** *disturb, agitate; tempt, attract, induce.* **vicinitas** *proximity.* **opportunitas** *convenience.* **mediocritas** *moderate size.* **avoco** *amuse.*

4 **scholasticus** *scholarly.* **porro** (adv.) *forward, onward, furthermore.* **tantum** *so much.* **soli** < **solum**, -i, n. *ground, land.* **relevare, reficere** *enjoy R&R.* **repto** *creep, crawl.* **limes**, -itis, m. *cross-path, boundary.* **semita** *path, by-way.* **tero** *rub, wear away.* **viticula** dim. of **vitis** *vine.* **arbuscula** *small arbor* (tree).

5 **quo magis** *so that ... more.* **nosse** = **novisse**. **dos**, dotis *dowry* > pl. *advantages.* quantum esset ille mihi [debiturus] [et] [quantum essem] ego tibi debiturus....

PART FOUR

SELECTIONS OF VARIOUS OTHER PEOPLE'S MAIL

These selections cover a very long span of time, from Cornelia mother of the Gracchi in the second century B.C.E. to Sidonius Apollinaris of the fifth century C.E. They include two women writers of letters: Cornelia, long admired for her literary style, and the barely literate Claudia Severa, writing an affectionate birthday party invitation to another officer's wife at their post near Hadrian's wall. Two emperors, a provincial bishop and two great poets of two distant times complete the list.

Cornelius Nepos, Fragment 59.1
A Letter of Cornelia to her son Gaius Gracchus

Cornelia was a heroic woman and legendary mother. She had given birth to twelve children of whom only three reached adulthood and only one survived her. Two who lived to maturity were the reformers Tiberius and Gaius Gracchus, and she is constantly referred to in antiquity as "mother of the Gracchi" (*Gracchorum mater*). By the time the letters to her son were written, Tiberius had already been assassinated. His brother Gaius was soon to follow.

A woman with stylus and writing tablet, after a Fayum-style painting from Pompeii in the Naples Archaeological Museum.

93

The authenticity of the two letters putatively addressed by Cornelia to her son Gaius is in dispute. She was praised for her style by both Atticus and Quintilian, which may account for the survival of her letters in antiquity whether or not these particular examples are genuine. The letters show the influence of mothers on even their grown sons' lives. The letters are preserved in *De Viris Illustribus*, a largely lost work of Cornelius Nepos, as fragments 1 and 2 (of which frag. 1 is excerpted for this collection). Cornelia's words are introduced with: *Verba ex epistula Corneliae Gracchorum matris ex libro Cornelii Nepotis de Latinis historicis excerpta*:

Dices pulchrum esse inimicos ulcisci. id neque maius neque pulchrius cuiquam atque mihi esse videtur, sed si liceat re publica salva ea persequi. sed quatenus id fieri non potest, multo tempore multisque partibus inimici nostri non peribunt atque, uti nunc sunt, erunt potius quam res publica profligetur atque pereat.

ulciscor -i, ultus/a sum *take vengeance on.* atque (conj.) *and, than, as.* re publica salva: abl. abs. of circumstance: "on condition that..." ea: neuter pl. object of persequi. quatenus (adv.) *insofar as.* multo tempore multisque partibus *much of the time and in a lot of places* or *respects;* or *a great deal.* erunt *will continue to be;* the subject is inimici. profligo (1) *destroy, overthrow, dash to the ground.*

Letter of Vergil to Augustus
Macrobius Saturnalia *1.24.11*

Ambrosius Theodosius Macrobius (4th-5th centuries C.E.) is the author of the *Saturnalia*, a fictionalized dialogue (or philosopical symposium) taking place on the three days of Saturnalia in December 384. It is a work of miscellaneous antiquarian lore with the poet Vergil as its central theme.

Ipsius enim Maronis epistola, qua conpellat Augustum, ita incipit:

Ego vero frequentes a te litteras accipio . . .

et infra:

De Aenea quidem meo, si mehercle iam dignum auribus haberem tuis, libenter mitterem: sed tanta inchoata res est, ut paene vitio mentis tantum opus ingressus mihi videar, cum praesertim, ut scis, alia quoque studia ad id opus multoque potiora inpertiar.

Augustus has been importuning Vergil for an outline and samples of the *Aeneid*, but the poet is now doubting his sanity in undertaking such a project and claiming that he needs to devote much more serious study to the epic.

According to Suetonius' *Vita Vergili* (39 ff.) before he left Italy for Greece, Vergil had made arrangements with Varius (who became his literary executor) to burn the *Aeneid*, should anything happen to him (*ut siquid sibi accidisset*, Aeneida *combureret*). On the return journey the poet fell ill and died, but Varius refused the dying man's request, and instead, at Augustus' insistence, published the work, even leaving the unfinished lines as they were (*versus etiam inperfectos sicut erant reliquerit*).

---

conpello (compello) (1) *address.* **et infra** *and below, further along* (i.e. later in the letter). **Aeneas**, -ae, m. (abl. **Aenea**) *Aeneas.* **mehercle** (interjection) *by Hercules, so help me Hercules.* [aliquid] **dignum. inchoo** (1) *begin* [Engl. *inchoate, inchoative* < **cohum/choum** *the strap used to attach the pole to the yoke*, orig. *the hollow in the center of the yoke into which the pole was fitted*, related to **cavus**, *hollow*]. **ingressus** [esse]. **praesertim** (adv.) *especially.* **inpertio** (**impertio**) *share, communicate, impart.*

Four Letters of Augustus

Letters of Augustus were kept in the imperial archives and owe their preservation to scholars who comment on them in their own works.

Letter of Augustus to his grandson Gaius (Aulus Gellius 15. 7. 3)

Aulus Gellius lived in the second century c.e. His work, the *Attic Nights*, was in twenty books, most of which is extant. He had studied literature in Rome and in his late twenties went to Athens for advanced work. During the winter nights he collected material for a series of short essays on "everything." This sort of miscellany of curious facts was popular in the ancient world and is coming back into vogue, as we see in such recent titles as *A Short History of Nearly Everything, The Meaning of Everything, Schott's Original Miscellany*. His reading and interests were varied, making the work very useful to us because of its preservation of so many facts and quotations from works otherwise lost to us.

Gellius introduces the letter by commenting on Augustus' style in the book of letters written to his grandson. "I was taken by the elegance of his style, neither mannered nor meticulous, but—by Hercules—easy and unaffected...."

IX KAL. OCTOBRIS
AVE, MI GAI,

Meus asellus iucundissimus, quem semper medius fidius
desidero, cum a me abes. Sed praecipue diebus talibus, qualis est
hodiernus, oculi mei requirunt meum Gaium, quem, ubicumque
hoc die fuisti, spero laetum et bene valentem celebrasse quartum
et sexagesimum natalem meum. Nam, ut vides, κλιμακτῆρα
communem seniorum omnium tertium et sexagesimum annum
evasimus.

Deos autem oro, ut mihi quantumcumque superest temporis,
id salvis nobis traducere liceat in statu rei publicae felicissimo,
ἀνδραγαθούντων ὑμῶν διαδεχομένων stationem meam.

IX Kal. Octobris = 23 September

Gaius, the grandson of Augustus, son of Julia and Agrippa. The plural in the last
line refers to Gaius and his brother Lucius. The boys were adopted by Augustus
and were designated as his successors.

asellus *donkey*; diminutive of **asinus**, used as a term of affection. See Suetonius *Life
of Augustus*, 62.3 on Augustus' treatment of his grandsons.

medius (me Dius) **fidius** "so help me god" **Dius fidius**, a title of Jupiter [cf.
mecastor, edepol, etc. *by Castor, by Pollux*]

κλιμακτῆρα < κλιμακτήρ the *rung* of a ladder; in Astrology, one of the
critical points in a person's life, occurring at seven year intervals (as 21, 28, 49, 63,
etc.) [cf. Engl. *climacteric*.]

On the climacteric, the introduction to this chapter of Gellius reads: *Observatum
esse in senibus quod annum fere aetatis tertium et sexagesimum agant aut laboribus
aut interitu aut clade aliqua insignitum: atque inibi super eadem observatione
exemplum adpositum epistulae divi Augusti ad Gaium filium.* "It has been observed
of the elderly that they pass their 63rd year marked by troubles or death or some
kind of catastrophe; and pertinent to this observation a copy of a letter of the
deified Augustus to his [grand]son Gaius is appended here."

ἀνδραγαθούντων ὑμῶν διαδεχομένων a genitive absolute "with you being
good men and succeeding to my position" [= **stationem meam**]. The plural
includes Gaius' brother Lucius.

Three Letters of Augustus quoted in Suetonius' *Life of Claudius* 3-4

Suetonius, the biographer of the Caesars, who held posts in the imperial archive, had access to the letters of Augustus and quotes several in his life of Claudius. These three letters were written to Livia, Augustus' wife. Excerpts from other letters of Augustus (concerned with gambling and eating habits) are found in Suetonius, *Life of Augustus* 71 and 76.

(3) Nam avunculus maior Augustus quid de eo in utramque partem opinatus sit, quo certius cognoscatur, capita ex ipsius epistulis posui.

(4.1) "Collocutus sum cum Tiberio, ut mandasti, mea Livia, quid nepoti tuo Tiberio faciendum esset ludis Martialibus. Consentit autem uterque nostrum, semel nobis esse statuendum, quod consilium in illo sequamur.

(2) Nam si est artius, ut ita dicam, holocleros, quid est quod dubitemus, quin per eosdem articulos et gradus producendus sit, per quos frater eius productus sit? Sin autem ἠλαττῶσθαι sentimus eum et βεβλάφθαι καὶ εἰς τὴν τοῦ σώματος καὶ εἰς τὴν τῆς ψυχῆς ἀρτιότητα, praebenda materia deridendi

---

3   **caput, -itis,** n. *head, main point;* pl. *summary.* **posui** *I have placed/appended.*

4.1   **Tiberius** 1. the future emperor *Tiberius,* Livia's son; **Tiberius** 2. the future emperor **Claudius,** Livia's grandson, son of Drusus and Antonia; his full name is Tiberius Claudius Drusus. Augustus was his great uncle (*avunculus maior*) through his sister Octavia, Claudius' grandmother. **ludis Martialibus:** the games to commemorate the dedication of the temple of Mars Ultor (the Avenger), built in fulfilment of a vow made by Augustus in the war at Philippi to avenge his (adoptive) father (Caesar), were held on the first of August. **nostrum:** gen. of **nos. semel** (adv.) *once for all.*

2   **artius** = ἄρτιος *complete, perfectly fitted.* **ut ita dicam** (idiom) *so to speak, if I may say so.* **holocleros** = ὁλόκληρος *complete, perfect* (with ἄρτιος: *with all his senses intact, in full control of his faculties*). **articulus, -i,** m. (dimin. of *artus*) *joint, clause, point.* **produco** *bring forward,* (of career or rank) *promote.* **frater:** Germanicus. Greek: ἠλαττῶσθαι (*to be diminished, be inferior*) and βεβλάφθαι (*to be harmed/disabled*): infinitives in indirect statement after **sentimus.** καὶ εἰς τὴν τοῦ σώματος καὶ εἰς τὴν τῆς ψυχῆς ἀρτιότητα: *both in the soundness of his body and that of his soul/character.*

et illum et nos non est hominibus τὰ τοιαῦτα σκώπτειν καὶ μυκτηρίζειν εἰωθόσιν.

(3) Nam semper aestuabimus, si de singulis articulis temporum deliberabimus, μὴ προυποκειμένου ἡμῖν posse arbitremur eum gerere honores necne. In praesentia tamen quibus de rebus consulis, curare eum ludis Martialibus triclinium sacerdotum non displicet nobis, si est passurus se ab Silvani filio homine sibi affini admoneri, ne quid faciat quod conspici et derideri possit.

(4) Spectare eum circenses ex pulvinari non placet nobis; expositus enim in fronte prima spectaculorum conspicietur. In Albanum montem ire eum non placet nobis aut esse Romae Latinarum diebus. Cur enim non praeficitur urbi, si potest sequi fratrem suum in montem?

(5) Habes nostras, mea Livia, sententias, quibus placet semel de tota re aliquid constitui, ne semper inter spem et metum fluctuemur. Licebit autem, si voles, Antoniae quoque nostrae des hanc partem epistulae huius legendam."

εἰωθόσιν: dat. with **hominibus**; τὰ τοιαῦτα σκώπτειν καὶ μυκτηρίζειν εἰωθόσιν: [to people who are] *in the habit of mocking and sneering at such things.*

3 **aestuo** (1) *burn fiercely, be agitated, be in an unsettled state of mind.* **singuli**, -ae, -a *one at a time.* Greek: μὴ προυποκειμένου ἡμῖν *if it is not laid down in advance.* **arbitremur**: subj. in indirect question with **necne** *whether or not.* **triclinium**, -i, n. *couches arranged on three sides with a central table for dining, dining couch, dining room.* **Silvani filius**: the son of Silvanus. M. Plautius Silvanus, to whose daughter, Plautia Urgulanilla, Claudius was engaged (see Suetonius *Claudius* 26.2) and with whose family the Claudii Nerones already had ties. Urgulanilla was Claudius' first wife, but he divorced her *ob libidinum probra et homocidii suspicionem.* **affinis**, -is, m. *relative by marriage.*

4 **pulvinar**, -aris, n. *a cushioned couch on which images of the gods were placed, sacred couch, seat of honor.* **Mons Albanus** the *Alban Mount* (= Monte Cavo). **Latinae**, -arum, f. pl. [feriae] a ceremony celebrated on the Mons Albanus by the peoples of Latium, annually on the Kalends of June (Livy 42.35.3). **praeficio** *put in charge* (of units of civil administration); here, the prefecture of the city.

5 **Antonia**: Claudius' mother.

(6) Rursus alteris litteris: "Tiberium adulescentem ego vero, dum tu aberis, cotidie invitabo ad cenam, ne solus cenet cum suo Sulpicio et Athenodoro. Qui vellem diligentius et minus μετέωρος deligeret sibi aliquem, cuius motum et habitum et incessum imitaretur. Misellus ἀτυχεῖ nam ἐν τοῖς σπουδαίοις ubi non aberravit eius animus, satis apparet ἡ τῆς ψυχῆς αὐτοῦ εὐγένεια."

(7) Item tertiis litteris: "Tiberium nepotem tuum placere mihi declamantem potuisse, peream nisi, mea Livia, admiror. Nam qui tam ἀσαφῶς loquatur, qui possit cum declamat σαφῶς dicere quae dicenda sunt, non video."

---

6   **Sulpicius:** Sulpicius Flavus, a friend of Claudius who, with the historian Livy, encouraged or helped him to write a history in his youth (Suetonius, *Claudius* 41). **Athenodorus** a freedman, friend of Claudius. μετέωρος *in midair; air-headed.* **deligo,** -ere *select, choose.* **incessus,** -us, m. *step, pace, gait.* **misellus:** diminutive of **miser.** ἀτυχεῖ *is unfortunate.* ἐν τοῖς σπουδαίοις *in serious matters.* ἡ τῆς ψυχῆς αὐτοῦ εὐγένεια: *his nobility/ generosity of spirit.*

7   **peream nisi** (idiom) *well, I'll be damned.* **qui** *how* (old ablative form). ἀ σαφῶς *unclearly.* σαφῶς *clearly.*

Two Letters of Trajan

Trajan (from Pliny *Epistulae* X.93)
Social clubs in Amisus

As Pliny traveled through his province, he wrote to his boss, Trajan, for advice about problems whose solutions were not immediately clear from law or precedent. Some of these concern legal and administrative matters, but some of the most interesting are about building and engineering projects. Trajan's answers could be considered progressive. He is in favor of improvements whether of civic, economic, or aesthetic conditions, provided the locals pay for them, they do not take anything from the imperial treasury, or offer opportunities for anti-imperial or anti-Roman activities. To what extent these rescripts were drafted by the imperial secretaries *ab epistulis* and how much input came from the emperor himself is undetermined, though we can be sure Trajan was not unconcerned with the policies discussed in these letters.

This rescript of Trajan is in response to Pliny's query (X.92) on behalf of the citizens of Amisus concerning ἔρανοι, societies for communal dining and/or mutual benefit, and sometimes for making loans to members. Two other replies from Trajan are found in Part Three with Pliny's requests.

TRAIANUS PLINIO

Amisenos, quorum libellum epistulae tuae iunxeras, si legibus istorum, quibus beneficio foederis utuntur, concessum est eranum habere, possumus quo minus habeant non impedire, eo facilius si tali collatione non ad turbas et ad illicitos coetus, sed ad sustinendam tenuiorum inopiam utuntur. In ceteris civitatibus, quae nostro iure obstrictae sunt, res huius modi prohibenda est.

Amiseni: the people of Amisus, a Greek settlement in Pontus; it was a free and federated community (*civitas libera et foederata*) which enjoyed the privilege of governing itself by its own laws. **libellus**, -i, m. *a small book, a formal communication, dispatch, a document containing a request.* **foedus**, -eris, n. *formal agreement, league, treaty.* **eranus**, -i, m. = Greek ἔρανος, a communal meal to which each person contributed to the cost. Trajan takes ἐράνους in Pliny's letter to mean the same as the Latin **collatio tenuiorum**, a social benefit club for the mutual welfare of the members. These were nominally connected with a religious cult and often made collections for the funeral expenses of members. **quo minus** depends on **impedire**, *from.* **collatio**, -onis, f. *placing together, fund raised by contributions.* **coetus**, -us, m. *meeting, union, gang.* Trajan was concerned about uprisings in the provinces and often refused permission to establish clubs, even turning down the establishment of a fire brigade. **tenuior**: comparative of **tenuis**, -e *thin, small, poor.* **inopia**, -ae, f. *lack of resources, poverty, helplessness.* **obstringo**, -ere, -nxi, -ctum *draw tight, bind, place under legal obligation.*

Trajan (from Pliny *Epistulae* X.97)
The Christians

One of Pliny's most famous letters (X.96) is the one in which he writes about the Christians who have been denounced to him. In his answer Trajan gives general approval of Pliny's course of action and declines to make any global decision for the empire as a whole, but as usual prefers to follow local custom (*neque in universum*). Pliny was not to accept anonymous denunciations nor to seek out Christians, but he could not ignore official information lodged.

TRAIANUS PLINIO S.

Actum quem debuisti, mi Secunde, in excutiendis causis eorum qui Christiani ad te delati fuerant secutus es. Neque enim in universum aliquid quod quasi certam formam habeat constitui potest. Conquirendi non sunt: si deferantur et arguantur, puniendi sunt, ita tamen ut qui negaverit se Christianum esse idque re ipsa manifestum fecerit, id est supplicando deis nostris, quamvis suspectus in praeteritum, veniam ex paenitentia inpetret. Sine auctore vero propositi libelli in nullo crimine locum habere debent. Nam et pessimi exempli nec nostri saeculi est.

---

actus, -us, m. *legal procedure, method.* **excutio,** -ere *investigate.* **defero,** -ferre, -tuli, -latum *convey, denounce, lay information;* cf. **delator** *informer.* **in universum** *in general.* **conquiro,** -ere *hunt, seek out.* **arguo,** -ere *prove guilty.* **in praeteritum** *into the past.* **venia,** -ae, f. *pardon, clemency.* **inpetro** (1) *obtain a request.* **sine auctore** *anonymous.* **libellus,** -i, m. *document;* here *denunciation.* **crimen,** -inis, n. *indictment, charge, accusation.* **pessimi exempli nec nostri saeculi**: predicate genitives of characteristic.

Vindolanda Letter of Claudia Severa

This fragment comes from the cache of letters found at Vindolanda, a Roman military installation in Britain. These letters are on thin strips of wood and written in ink. The first part of the text, a birthday invitation, was written by a professional scribe but lines 11-14 were probably written by Claudia Severa herself (just as one often adds a personal message to a special friend to a printed card or invitation), making this possibly the earliest actual identifiable example of a woman's handwriting in Latin. The strips were folded, forming a kind of note card. The back contains the address and return address. The text is based on that of Alan K. Bowman and J. David Thomas (*Britannia* 18:137-40 and Plate xvi, 1987).

left side (lines 1-6)

Cl Seuera Lepidinae [suae]
[sa]l[u]tem
Iii Idus septembr[e]s soror ad diem
sollemnem natalem meum rogo
libenter facias ut uenias[.]   5
ad nos iucundiorem mihi

---

1 Cl = Claudia. She was the wife of Aelius Brocchus.

2 **salutem** is the traditional greeting (or salutation) in a Roman letter (See introduction page 6).

3 **iii Id. Septembres.** *September 11.*

4 **sollemnis, -e** *appointed, for celebration*: **ad diem sollemnem natalem meum** *to my birthday party.* **rogo** "I invite you" is equivalent to "you are invited"

5 **libenter** *gladly, sincerely, cordially* (adverb with **rogo**). **facias**: jussive noun clause with **rogo**. **ut venias**: substantive clause of result with **facias**.

6 **iucundus, -a, -um** *pleasant, agreeable.*

right side (lines 7-14)

> [diem] interuentu tuo factura si
> > [uenie]s[.]
>
> Cerial[em tu]um saluta Aelius meus
> > et filiolus salutant   10
> > sperabo te soror
> > uale soror anima
> > mea ita ualeam
> > karissima et haue

back (address and return address)

> Sulpicae Lepidinae   15
> [Flaui]i Cerialis
> [a Se]uera

7   **interventus, -us, m.** *arrival, attendance, coming.* **factura [es]** is equivalent to **facies** in a future more vivid condition.

9   **saluta:** imperative "Say hi to..." **Cerialem:** Cerialis is Sulpicia Lepidina's husband. **Aelius** is Claudia's husband.

10   **filiolus** diminutive of **filius. salutant** *send their greetings.*

11   The four lines (111-14) are in her own hand. **sperabo te** *I will expect you.* "I'm looking forward to seeing you."

12-14   **vale ... ita valeam** perhaps a variation of **si vales bene est ego valeo** (a common formula in letters; see note on Cicero XIV.21. "Be well, so may I be well." Claudia then uses **have** (= **ave** instead of the usual **vale**) as her closing (or valediction). **karissima = carissima.**

16   **Flavii Cerialis** *wife of Flavius Cerialis* (*Mrs. Flavius Cerialis*)

See Vindolanda Tablets Online http://vindolanda.csad.ox.ac.uk/tablets/ Tablet 291.

Ausonius, *Epistulae* xxii
A poem for his grandson

Decimus Magnus Ausonius was born in Bordeaux in 310 c.e., spent thirty years as a teacher, and through his literary skill rose to prominence. He was a prolific poet, composing in many meters and styles and on a great variety of subjects. His most famous poem was *Mosella*, a praise of the river Moselle and its fish, fishermen, and other features. About two dozen of his letters survive, mostly in verse, but a few in prose. The most important are to Paulinus of Nola, but this brief example to his son Hesperius reveals a kindly and charming personality. Ausonius was a life-long Christian.

Ausonius Hesperio Filio

(1) Libellum, quem ad nepotulum meum, sororis tuae filium, instar protreptici luseram, venturus ipse praemisi legendum. Hoc enim malui quam ipse recitare, esset ut tibi censura liberior, quae duabus causis impediri solet: quod aures nostras audita velocius quam lecta praetereunt et quod sinceritas iudicandi praesentia recitantis oneratur. Nunc tibi utrumque integrum est, quia et legenti libera mora est et iudicaturo non obstat nostri verecundia.

---

1   **nepotulus**, -i, m. dimin. of **nepos**, -otis, m. *grandson* [> Engl. *nepotism, nephew*]. Diminutives are common in later Latin. Here they are especially appropriate to the subject, the sending of a poem to a child. **instar** (indecl. noun) *likeness*. **protrepticon**/um, -i, n. *a hortatory discourse*, originally an exhortation to philosophy but here in a much lighter vein. **ludo**, ere, lusi, lusum *play; write light verse*. The poem is attached to the letter, but not included here. **censura**, -ae f. *censorship, criticism*. **praetereo**, -ire, -ii/ivi, -itum *go past, pass*. **praesentia**: ablative. **integer**, -gra, -grum *whole, complete, unbiased*. **nostri**: gen. of **nos**, objective gen. with **verecundia**. **verecundia**, -ae, f. *modesty, reverence*.

(2) Set heus tu, fili dulcissime, habeo quod admoneam. Si qua tibi in his versiculis videbuntur (nam vereor, ut multa sint) fucatius concinnata quam verius et plus coloris quam suci habere, ipse sciens fluere permisi, venustula ut essent magis quam forticula, instar virginum, quas matres student demissis umeris esse, vincto pectore, ut graciles sient.

(3) Nosti cetera. Superest igitur, ut dicas: "quid moraris iudicationem meam de eo, quod ipse pronuntias esse mendosum?" Dicam scilicet me huiusmodi versibus foris erubescere, set intra nos minus verecundari: namque ego haec annis illius magis quam meis scripsi aut fortasse et meis: δὶς παῖδες οἱ γέροντες. Ad summam valeat austeritas tua: mihi cum infante ratio est.

Vale, fili dulcissime.

---

2   **set** = **sed. heus** (interjection) *ho, yo, hey*. **fucatius**: compar. adv. of **fucatus**, -a, -um *counterfeit, artificial*; perf. pass. participle of **fuco** (1) *paint, dye*. **concinno** (1) *arrange*. **sucus**, -i, m. *juice, sap* (i.e. *life, vigor*) [> Engl. *succulent*]. **venustulus**, -a, -um dimin. of **venustus** [< **Venus**] *charming*. **forticulus**, -a, -um dimin. of **fortis** *fairly brave/strong*. **quas ... sient**: Terence, *Eunuchus*, 313-14. **studeo** (with infinitive) *strive after, take pains for*. **demitto**, -ere, -misi, -missum *let down, lower*. **umerus**, -i, m. *shoulder*. **vincio**, -ire, vinxi, vinctum *bind* (with a corset). **gracilis**, -e *slender*.

3   **nosti** = **novisti. superest** *it remains* (see Pliny I.1). **moror** (1, depon.) *delay, await*. **mendosus**, -a, -um *full of faults* [> Engl. *emend*]. **scilicet** (adv.) *you may be sure, of course* [< scire licet]. **foris** (adv.) *out of doors, abroad, to other people* [Engl. words from this root include *forum, foreign, forest, forensic*]. **erubesco**, -ere, -rubui *blush*. **annis**: dat. ("for"). **illius** = his grandson, Ausonius. δὶς παῖδες οἱ γέροντες: Greek proverb: "old men are twice children." **ad summam** *on the whole, in short*. **mihi**: dat. of possession. **ratio**, -onis, f. *affair, business, concern*.

Sidonius VII. 18
The letters are ready

For a wealthy provincial aristocrat, Gaius Sollius Sidonius Apollinaris had a life full of incident. He was born about 430 C.E. of Gallo-Roman stock. He married Papianilla, daughter of Avitus who was proclaimed emperor of the western Roman empire in 455. Among the vicissitudes that followed this major event are the fall of Avitus, changes in government, imperial posts, election to the bishopric of Auvergne, imprisoment after Rome gave up Auvergne to Euric the Visigoth King, and ultimate restoration to his See. He delivered panegyrics of over 500 lines of verse each in honor of three emperors, wrote twenty-four books of poems and nine books of letters. In 486 he died and was later canonized (his feast day being on August 21). His style is annoying, but endearing for that very reason, with its made-up words (not found in the classical Latin word stock) and over-indulgence in preciosity of word play, verbal jingles, and complicated contrasts.

SIDONIUS CONSTANTIO SUO SALUTEM

(1) A te principium, tibi desinet. nam petitum misimus opus raptim electis exemplaribus, quae ob hoc in manus pauca venerunt, quia mihi nil de libelli huiusce conscriptione meditanti hactenus incustodita nequeunt inveniri. sane ista pauca, quae quidem et levia sunt, celeriter absolvi, quamquam incitatus semel animus necdum scripturire desineret, servans hoc sedulo genus

---

This was meant to be the last letter in Sidonius' collection, but more friends wanted to be included and persuaded him to add two more books.

Constantius was a priest whom Sidonius admired for his character and ability. Letter I.1 is also addressed to Constantius who had asked Sidonius to publish his letters, to which he replies:

> Diu praecipis... ut si quae mihi litterae paulo politiores varia occasione fluxerint, prout eas causa persona tempus elicuit, omnes retractatis exemplaribus enucleatisque uno volumine includam, Quinti Symmachi rotunditatem, Gai Plinii disciplinam maturitatemque vestigiis presumptuosis insecaturus.

Following Pliny's example, Sidonius revised his letters for publication and kept their subject to a single theme.

1   **A te principium**: Vergil, *Ecl.* 8.11. **raptim** (adv.) *hastily, hurriedly.* **ob hoc** points ahead to **quia**. **hactenus** (adv.) *thus far, until now.* **incustoditus**, -a, -um *not watched over carefully, neglected, not diligently preserved.* **nequeo**, -ere *be unable, cannot.* **necdum** (conj.) *and not yet.* **scripturio**, -ire *tend to write, enjoy writing, be eager to write*; Sidonius is fond of using verbs coined from nouns and adjectives. **sedulo** (adv.) *busily, diligently.*

temperamenti, ut epistularum produceretur textus, si numerus breviaretur.

(2) Pariter et censui librum, quem lector delicatissimus desiderares, et satis habilem nec parum excusabilem fore, si, quoniam te sensuum structurarumque levitas poterat offendere, membranarum certe fascibus minus onerarere. commendo igitur varios iudicio tuo nostri pectoris motus, minime ignarus, quod ita mens pateat in libro velut vultus in speculo. dictavi enim quaepiam hortando, laudando plurima et aliqua suadendo, maerendo pauca iocandoque nonnulla.

(3) Et si me uspiam lectitavisti in aliquos concitatiorem, scias volo Christi dextera opitulante me numquam toleraturum animi servitutem, compertissimum tenens bipertitam super his moribus hominum esse censuram. nam ut timidi me temerarium, ita constantes liberum appellant. inter quae ipse decerno satis illius iacere personam, cuius necesse est latere sententiam.

(4) Ad propositum redeo. interea tu, si quid a lectionis sacrae continuatione respiras, his licebit neniis avocere. nec faciet materia ut immensa fastidium, quia cum singulae causae singulis ferme epistulis finiantur, cito cognitis in quae oculum intenderis ante legere cessabis quam lecturire desistas. vale.

---

temperamentum, -i, n. *proportion, balanced admixture, moderation; compensating sense of balance* (Loeb translation). **produco** *lead forth, lengthen*. **brevio** (1) *shorten* (a neologism).

2   **habilis**, -e *handy*. **membrana**, -ae, f. *skin, parchment* [which had replaced papyrus as the writing material of choice]. **fascis**, -is, m. *bundle, packet*. **motus**, -us, m. *moving, impulse, passion*. **minime ignarus**: litotes (the statement of something by the denial of its opposite). **minime** (adv.) *not at all*. **dicto** (1) *compose*. The gerunds **hortando, laudando**, etc. are dative of purpose. **maereo**, -ere *mourn, lament*.

3   **concitatus**, -a, -um (< **concito**) *rapid, swift*. **dextera** (**dextra**), -ae, f. *right hand*. **opitulor** (1, depon.) *bring aid, succor*. **compertus**, -a, -um (< **comperio**) *clearly known*. **bipertitus** (**bipartitus**) *divided*. **temerarius**, -a, -um *rash, heedless* [> Engl. *temerarious, temerity*].

4   **propositum**, -i, n. *that which is proposed, main point, theme*. **continuatio**, -onis, f. *prolonging, uninterrupted practice*. **respiro** (1) *breathe back, be relieved, pause, take a break*. **nenia**, -ae, f. *song at a funeral; song, charm*; pl. *silly things*. **lecturio**, -ire *tend to read, enjoy reading, be passionately fond of reading*.

GRAMMAR REVIEWS

A. Review of Cases

With examples mostly from the letters of Cicero and Pliny the Younger (Those from letters not in this collection are translated.)

GENITIVE CASE (A&G 341-359)

I. Endings

I	-ae, -arum
II	-i, -orum
III	-is, -um, -ium
IV	-us, -uum
V	-ei, -erum

II. Meaning and Use in general: The genitive case generally expresses the relation of one noun to another, and is therefore an *adjectival* case (as opposed to the dative and ablative which are adverbial) because its most common function is to define or complete the meaning of another noun on which it depends. **The genitive is the case of one noun depending on another.**

III. Uses with examples from Pliny's and Cicero's letters:

1-4 GENITIVE WITH NOUNS

1. Possessive Genitive: denotes the person or thing to which an object, quality, action, or feeling belongs.

Proxime cum in patria mea fui, venit ad me salutandum *municipis mei* filius praetextatus.   Pliny IV.13.

Et pater *eius* (erat enim una atque etiam ipse adduxerat puerum) quia nullos hic praeceptores habemus.   Pliny IV.13.

> **Note** that for personal pronouns (of the first and second persons and the third person reflexive) possession is expressed by the possessive adjectives in agreement with their nouns (rather than by the possessive genitive of the adjective or pronoun: compare *meus, noster, tuus, vester, suus* to the use of *eius, eorum, earum*).

2. **Genitive of Quality, Description, or Characteristic** is used only when the quality is modified by an adjective. The genitive of quality is much less common in classical prose than the ablative of quality. In general the genitive of quality is used of **essential**, the ablative of quality of **special** or **incidental** characteristics. [A&G 345]

> Erat sane *somni paratissimi*, non numquam etiam inter ipsa studia *instantis* et *deserentis*.   Pliny III.5
>
> *quantae* mihi *curae* fuerit ...   Cicero *ad Att.* I.5.

Expressions such as *eius modi, cuius modi* are genitive of quality.

The **genitive of measure** is a type of genitive of quality used with numerals.

Another variety of the genitive of quality is the **genitive of price** or **value** (cf also the genitive of **charge** or **penalty** with verbs of accusing, condemning or acquitting).

> Tu modo enitere ut tibi ipse sis *tanti quanti* videberis aliis si tibi fueris.   Pliny I.3.

3. **Objective Genitive**: used for the object of an emotion, action, or agency.

> E.g. *amor patris* may mean:
>   1. "a father's love" – subjective genitive
>   2. "love for a father" – objective genitive

> Tanta erat parsimonia *temporis*.   Pliny III.5.
>
> *tui*que et sua sponte et meo sermone amantem adfinem amicumque amiseris.   Cicero *Ad Att.* I.5

4. **Partitive Genitive**: the whole of which a part is taken or identified goes into the genitive [also called the genitive of the whole]. The partitive genitive is especially common with indefinite pronouns and with comparatives and superlatives.

> Surgebat aestate a cena luce, hieme intra primam *noctis*.   Pliny III.5.
>
> Post cibum saepe, quem interdiu levem et facilem veterum more sumebat, aestate, si quid *otii*, iacebat in sole, liber legebatur, adnotabat excerpebatque.   Pliny III.5.
>
> nihil *litterarum* ...   Cicero *ad Att.* I.2.

5. GENITIVE WITH ADJECTIVES

Adjectives denoting *desire, knowledge, memory, fullness, power, sharing, guilt* [and their opposites] may take the genitive.

> *partium* studiosus   Cicero *ad Att.* I.13. ["full of years, full of honors"]

>> **Note:** *plenus* "full of" may also take the ablative: *plenus annis, plenus honoribus.*   Pliny II.1

The genitive is used with adjectives in -**ax** in poetry and Later Latin.

6. GENITIVE WITH VERBS

Verbs of accusing, condemning and acquitting take the genitive of the charge or penalty. Verbs of remembering and forgetting take the genitive. Verbs of reminding take the genitive of the thing and the accusative of the person.

> Sed tu, qui *huius iudicii* meministi, cur *illius* oblitus es
> in quo me interrogasti quid de Meti Modesti pietate
> sentirem?   Pliny I.5

Verbs of feeling take the genitive of the object which excites the feeling [objective genitive].

The impersonals: **miseret**, *pity*; **paenitet**, *regret*; **piget**, *disgust*; **pudet**, *shame*; **taedet**, *tire, weary* take the genitive of the cause of the feeling and the accusative of the person affected by the feeling. *Interest* and *refert* may also take the genitive of the person affected.

> Superest ut nec te *consilii* nec me paeniteat *obsequii*.   Pliny I.1

EXERCISES

Translate:
1. The son of Pliny's friend is a student [i.e. studies] in Milan.
2. His father said that the boy had no teachers.
3. My uncle was a man of the most grave character.
4. Fannia was a woman of ancient virtue.
5. Regulus is the worst of all informers.
6. What did Regulus forget?
7. Do you have any leisure?
8. Do we regret our advice?

Dative Case (A&G 360-385)

I. Endings

I	-ae, -is
II	-o, -is
III	-i, -ibus
IV	-ui/-u -ibus
V	-ei, -ebus

II. General Uses:

1. An object not caused by the action or directly affected by it, but sharing in it or receiving it.

2. The purpose of an action or that for which it serves.

   The dative case indicates the person or thing interested in the state or action described by the verb. Many relations expressed by the dative in Latin are expressed by **to** or **for** in English (though English, too, often omits the preposition). The difference between the accusative and dative often depends upon the point of view implied in the verb or existing in the mind of the speaker or writer. (A&G 360)

III. Uses of the dative with examples:

1. **Indirect Object**: some transitive verbs, especially verbs of giving, showing, telling, entrusting, take an accusative of the direct object and a **dative** of the **indirect** object.

   Quin tu (tempus est enim) humiles et sordidas curas *aliis* mandas et ipse te in alto isto pinguique secessu *studiis* adseris?   Pliny I.3.

   dixerit *ei* Metius Carus ...   Pliny I.5.

   quod *mihi* mandaras ...   Cicero *ad Att.* I.5.

   > **Note** that in the passive the dative remains dative [though what would have been the object in the active becomes the subject in the passive].

2. **Dative with "Special Verbs"** = Dative with Intransitive Verbs

   The Latin equivalents of many transitive English verbs are intransitive. Many of these take a **dative** object rather than an accusative. That is, they complete their meaning with an indirect object, as if the idea of the direct object is already contained in the verb itself. Verbs of *aiding, favoring, obeying, pleasing,* and *serving*; verbs of *injuring, opposing, displeasing*; verbs of *commanding, persuading, trusting, distrusting, sparing, pardoning, envying, being angry* take the **dative** case.

   Some of the most common of these Latin verbs are:

   faveo *favor*; **studeo** *desire* [have zeal, enthusiasm for]; **credo** *believe* [put one's faith in]; **consulo** *consult for* (with acc. *consult, ask advice* *of*); **cedo** *yield to*; **impero** *command, order, rule*; **minor, minitor** *threaten*; **fido, confido** *trust* [put one's trust in]; diffido, distrust; **suadeo, persuadeo** *persuade* [make a thing sweet to]; **noceo** *harm* [do a hurt to]; **parco** *spare*; **indulgeo** *indulge*; **irascor** *be angry at*; **pareo** *obey*; **servio** *serve*; **invideo** *envy* [look askance at]; **placeo** *please*; **ignosco** *pardon*; **respondeo** *answer*; **evenio** *happen*.

The dative is also used with the **impersonals** *licet* (it is permitted) and *libet/lubet* (it pleases).

servi *valetudini* ...   Cicero *ad Fam*. XIV.2.

ideo nihil alterutrum in partem respondere *tibi* possum ... Pliny I.5

cum responderet *mihi* et *Satrio Rufo*.   Pliny I.5

Coepit vereri ne *sibi* irascerer; nec fallebatur, irascebar. Pliny I.5

"Interrogavi, non ut *tibi* nocerem, sed ut *Modesto*." Vide hominis crudelitatem, qui se non dissimulet *exuli* nocere voluisse.   Pliny I.5

> **Notes:**
> 1. In the passive, these verbs are used impersonally:
>> *mihi persuadetur* "it is persuaded to me" = I am persuaded
>> *tibi diffiditur* "it is distrusted to you" = you are distrusted
> 2. Some exceptions to the general rule about the types of verbs that take the dative are: *iubeo, delector, iuvo, hortor, laedo, offendo* which take the accusative.

3. Dative with Compound Verbs: many verbs compounded with *ad, ante, con, in, inter, ob, post, prae, pro, sub, super* and some with *circum* take the dative.
> **Note**: if the verb is transitive, a direct object may also be found.

> qui tota vita *litteris* adsident.   Pliny III.5.

> experieris non Dianam magis *montibus* quam Minervam inerrare.   Pliny I.6. ["You will find that Diana does not wander the mountains any more than Minerva."]

> Triginta annis *gloriae suae* supervixit ... et *posteritati suae* interfuit.   Pliny II.1.

4. Dative with Adjectives: the dative is used with adjectives (and even with adverbs) for the person or thing affected by the quality which the adjective denotes (cf. dative with compound verbs). Such adjectives include those expressing: *advantage, disadvantage, usefulness, fitness, facility, nearness, dearness* and their opposites.

Some adjectives that take the dative:

Fitness: **idoneus** *suitable for;* **aptus** *fitted to [/ + ad + acc.];*
   accommodatus *suited to [/ + ad + acc.];* **utilis** *useful to [/ + ad +*
   acc.]; **inutilis** *useless for [/ + ad + acc.].*

Likeness: **similis** *like [/ + gen. of person];* **dissimilis** *unlike;* **par** *equal to*
   [/ + gen.]; **aequus** *equal to;* **iniquus** *unequal to;* **proprius** *peculiar to*
   [/ + gen.]; **communis** *common to [/ + gen.].*

Nearness: **proximus** *next to, nearest;* **finitimus** *neighboring to*

Friendliness: **amicus** *friendly to;* **inimicus** *unfriendly, hostile to;* **carus**
   dear to; **infestus** *hostile to;* **gratus** *pleasing to;* **adversus** *opposed to,*
   facing; **contrarius** *opposed to, opposite.*

Pergratum est *mihi* quod tam diligenter libros avunculi mei
lectitas ut habere velis quaerasque qui sint omnes.   Pliny
III.5.

Fungar indicis partibus atque etiam quo sint ordine scripti
notum tibi faciam: est enim haec quoque *studiosis* non
iniucunda cognitio.   Pliny III.5.

Confido tamen haec quoque *tibi* non minus grata quam ipsos
libros futura, quae te non tantum ad legendos eos verum
etiam ad simile aliquid elaborandum possunt aemulationis
stimulis excitare.   Pliny III.5.

non dubito quin *tibi* quoque id molestum sit   Cicero *ad Att.*
I.5.

5. **Dative of Possession**: The dative is used for the **possessor** with forms of *esse*
   when more emphasis is to be put on the thing possessed than on the possessor,
   or on the interest of the possessor in the thing possessed. The thing possessed
   is the subject of this construction.

   Est enim, inquam, *mihi* cum Cicerone aemulatio, nec sum
   contentus eloquentia saeculi nostri.   Pliny I.5

6. **The Dative of Agent**: The dative is used of the agent with the gerundive + *sum*
   (the future passive periphrastic) to denote the person on whom the obligation
   rests. The dative of agent is common with perfect participles, especially when
   used in an adjectival sense and is used by poets and Silver Age writers with
   almost any passive form.

   quid sit *vobis* faciendum ...   Cicero *ad Fam.* XIV.14.

The dative of the person who sees or thinks is regularly used after *videor,*
"seem".

   Nonne videtur *tibi recordanti* quantum legerit, quantum
   scripsisset, nec in officiis ullis nec in amicitia principis

fuisse, rursus, cum audis quid studiis laboris inpenderit, nec scripsisse satis nec legisse?   Pliny III.5.

7. **The Dative of Reference** or **Interest** denotes the person interested: the person or thing for whose benefit or to whose prejudice the action is performed. This dative (also called the dative of advantage or disadvantage: *dativus commodi aut discommodi*) depends not on a particular word but on the general meaning of the construction. This dative is often used of the person from whose point of view an opinion is stated or a situation or direction is defined. Under this heading come "the dative of the local standpoint," "the dative of the person judging," "the ethical dative," and "the dative of separation."

Hic fere *nobis* sermonis terminus.   Pliny I.5.

Tu modo enitere ut *tibi* ipse sis tanti quanti videberis aliis si *tibi* fueris.   Pliny I.3.

Quod evenit mihi, postquam in Laurentino meo aut lego aliquid aut scribo aut etiam *corpori* vaco, cuius fulturis animus sustinetur.   Pliny I.9.

A variety of the dative of reference is the **ethical dative** which is used of the personal pronouns to show some interest on the part of the person indicated.

Ecce *tibi* Regulus "quaero" inquit, "Secunde, quid de Modesto sentias."   Pliny I.5.

The **Dative of Separation** may also be considered a variety of the dative of reference or interest: verbs of *taking away* may take the dative (especially of a person) instead of the ablative of separation. In Pliny this is not confined to persons as it is in earlier Latin.

Doleo enim feminam maximam eripi *oculis* civitatis, nescio an aliquid simile *visuris*.   Pliny VII.19.

8. **The Dative of Purpose** denotes that for which something serves. This is common in combination with the dative of reference in the **double dative**.

Hanc ego vitam voto et cogitatione praesumo, ingressurus avidissime, ut primum ratio aetatis *receptui* canere permiserit.   Pliny III.1 ["I anticipate this life with prayer and reflection, intending to set out upon it with relish as soon as considerations of age permit [me] *to sound the trumpet for retreat.*]

maximo te mihi *usui* fore video.   Cicero, *ad Att.* I.2

EXERCISES

Translate:
1. Will Caninius Rufus entrust the cares of his estate to his slaves?
2. What did Mettius Carus say to Regulus?
3. Regulus wished to reconcile Pliny to himself.
4. He did not have a son.
5. Why was Pliny angry with Regulus?
6. It is pleasing to Pliny that we keep reading his letters.
7. Regulus wished to harm Modestus.
8. What mask will you put on (yourself)?

ACCUSATIVE CASE (386-399)

I. Endings

I	-am	-as
II	-um	-os -a
III	-em,-e,-al,-ar,-us	-es,-is/-ā
IV	-um,-u	-us,-ua
V	-em	-es

II. Uses with examples:

1. **Direct object** of a transitive verb: that which is directly affected or that which is caused or produced by the action of the verb.

   > Frequenter hortatus es ut *epistulas, siquas* paulo curatius scripsissem, colligerem publicaremque.   Pliny I.1

   In Silver Age Latin the accusative is used after *audire* and *cogitare* instead of *de* + the ablative.

   > *Verginium* cogito, Verginium video, Verginium iam vanis imaginibus, recentibus tamen, audio, adloquor, teneo.
   > Pliny I.12 ["I think Verginius, I see Verginius — Verginius in apparitions now empty, but still fresh, I hear, address, hold."]

   Impersonals with the accusative.

   > **decet**: Exponit Reguli mandata, addit preces suas, ut decebat *optimum virum* pro dissimillimo, parce.   Pliny I.5

   > **paenitet**: superest ut nec *te* paeniteat consilii nec *me* paeniteat obsequii.   Pliny I.1

2. **Cognate Accusative**: an intransitive verb often takes the accusative of a noun of kindred meaning, or the accusative of a neuter pronoun or adjective of indefinite reference.

   > *vitam vivere*   "to live a life"

Refert tamen *eventura* soleas an *contraria* somniare.   Pliny
I.18 ["Nevertheless, it makes a difference whether you are
accustomed to dream things that are about to take place or
their opposites."]

TWO ACCUSATIVE WITH ONE VERB

3. **The Predicate Accusative** refers to the same person or object as the direct
object, but is not in apposition to it. This is found with verbs of *choosing,
making, esteeming, showing.* If changed to the passive voice, this **predicate
accusative** becomes the predicate nominative.

> ... in quo Rusticum insectatur atque etiam Stoicorum *simiam*
> appellat.   Pliny I.5.
>
>> In the passive this would be ... Rusticus appellatur Stoicorum
>> *simia.*

4. **Secondary Object**
> a. With compounds of transitive verbs, the secondary object was
> originally governed by the preposition of the compound [see A&G
> 395].
>
> b. Verbs of *asking, teaching, concealing* may take two accusatives, one
> of the person [= direct object], one of the thing [= the secondary
> object]. In the passive, the secondary object remains accusative.
> [A&G 396]

5. **Adverbial Uses of the Accusative**
With *interest* and *refert* the degree of interest is expressed by an adverbial
accusative.

> *Plurimum* refert quid esse tribunatum putes...   Pliny I.23.
> ["It makes a big difference what you think the tribunate is."]

6. **Accusative of Specification** (Greek accusative or accusative of respect);
accusative of the part affected.

> *Hoc* tamen differunt...   Pliny I.4 ["they differ in this
> respect"]

7. **Accusative of Exclamation** ["such expressions depend upon a long-forgotten
verb" A&G 397d]

> O *rectam sinceramque vitam, o dulce otium honestum*que ac
> paene omni negotio *pulchrius.*   Pliny I.9.

8. **Accusative as subject of an Infinitive**: the subject of an infinitive is accusative;
this construction is especially common after verbs of *thinking, knowing, telling,
perceiving*, in indirect statement.

> posse enim iuvenem   Pliny VI.20 ["that [I] as a young
> person could..."]

Ludere *me* putas? Pliny I.11 ["You think I'm kidding?"]

9. Accusative of Extent of Space, Duration of Time.

cum *multos dies* auris meas Acutilio dedissem Cicero *ad Att.* I.5.

In Silver Age Latin duration of time goes into the ablative.

qui *tota vita* litteris adsident. Pliny III.5.

10. Place to which (=Terminal Accusative) with *ad, in.* With the names of towns and small islands and with *domum* and *rus* the preposition is omitted. In poetry the preposition is also often omitted.

Regressi *Misenum* ... Pliny VI.20.

Romam veni ... Cicero *ad Att.* I.5.

EXERCISES

Translate:

1. Pliny says that his letters have been written with a bit more care.
2. Pliny went to Corellius while he [Corellius] was abstaining from food [cibum].
3. Pliny does not regret his advice.
4. Suetonius dreamed [somnio(1)] strange things.
5. Pliny called Metius Modestus a peach of a fellow [i.e. a/the best man].

ABLATIVE CASE (398-422)

I. Endings

I	-a,	-is
II	-o,	-is
III	-e,-I	-ibus
IV	-u	-ibus
V	-e	-ebus

II. Uses in General

The functions of the Latin Ablative cover three relationships: **Ablative** (*from*); **Locative** (*in*); and **Instrumental** (*by, with*).

III. **Uses with examples:**

A. ABLATIVE (SEPARATIVE): FROM

1. Separation
a. with *ab, ex, de*

nondum *ab exilio* venerat.   Pliny I.5.

The ablative with *e/ex* or *de* is used with numbers (except *milia*) and with *quidam* instead of the partitive genitive.

unus *ex multis*   Pliny I.3.

b. With verbs of *departing, removing, depriving, freeing, robbing, abstaining, lacking*; with adjectives such as *liber, nudus, vacuus*, the ablative is used **without a preposition.**

Sinopenses, domine, *aqua* deficiuntur ...   Pliny X.90.

2. Source: that from which a thing is derived (usually with *ab, ex, de*); or the material of which it consists (with *ex*). But participles of birth or origin take the ablative of source without a preposition.

nuntius *a Spurrina*   Pliny I.5.

3. Cause: with or without a preposition [*ab, ex, de*], the motive that influences the mind of the person acting is expressed by the ablative of cause. The ablative of cause is used especially with verbs or adjectives denoting mental states.

exultaverat *morte*.   Pliny I.5.

rogatu Aruleni Rustici   Pliny I.5.

qui contentus est *eloquentia* saeculi nostri   Pliny I.5.

intentione rei familiaris obeundae   Pliny I.3. ["by reason of your effort in attending to your estate."]

conscientia exterritus   Pliny I.5.

Haec ad te pluribus verbis scripsi, quam soleo, non otii *abundantia*, sed amoris erga te.   Cicero *ad Fam.* VII.1.

4. Agent: the voluntary agent after a passive verb is expressed by the ablative with *a/ab*.

a Domitiano relegatus   Pliny I.5. ["sentenced by Domitian."]

te decipi *a me* non oportet   Pliny I.5.

curatur *a multis*, timetur *a pluribus*   Pliny I.5.

abs te accusor   Cicero, *ad Att.* I.5.

The ablative of **agent** is a development of the ablative of source: the agent being the source or author of the action.

5. **Comparison**: after a comparative adjective or other word implying comparison, the ablative is used to mean **than**.

> *Populo* vero nihil fortius ...   Cicero *ad Fam.* XII.4.

> vidistine quemquam *M. Regulo* timidiorem?   Pliny I.5.

> quod plerumque fortius *amore* est...   Pliny I.5.

> *omni negotio* pulchrius   Pliny I.9.

>> **Note:** the comparative may also be followed by *quam* (than) and the two things compared are put into the same case. The *quam* construction is always used when the first of the things compared is in any case other than the nominative or the accusative.

B. Instrumental Ablative: BY, WITH

The uses of the ablative for *means, instrument, manner* and *accompaniment* (some of these uses with, others without, a preposition) are derived from the old instrumental case. "No sharp lines can be drawn between them, and indeed the Romans themselves can hardly have thought of any distinction." [A&G 408]

1. Means or Instrument

> cuius *fulturis* animus sustinetur ...   Pliny I.9. ["by the maintenance of which the spirit is sustained."]

> quod nec famam meam *aliquo responso, utili* fortasse, *inhonesto* tamen, laeseram   Pliny I.5.

> Haec ad te *pluribus verbis* scripsi, quam soleo ...   Cicero *ad Fam.* VII.1.

2. The deponent verbs *utor* (use, avail oneself of), *fruor* (enjoy), *fungor* (perform), *potior* (take possession of), *vescor* (feed on) and some of their compounds take the ablative.

> Fungar indicis partibus ...   Pliny III.5.

This use of the ablative is *means*, with deponent verbs that imply the middle voice:

utor	"I employ myself by means of" > I use
fruor	"I enjoy myself by means of"
fungor	"I busy myself with" > I perform
vescor	"I feed myself with"
potior	"I make myself powerful with"

3. Also **nitor** (rest on, rely on; i.e. "I support myself by means of") and the adjective *fretus* (relying on) take an ablative of means.

> nitebamur ... *sententia* Meti Modestus   Pliny I.5.

4. **Opus est** (and sometimes *usus est*) "there is need of" takes an ablative of means. *Opus est*: literally "there is work" + the ablative of that by which the work is to be performed.

> *tuis* opus non est.   Pliny I.4 ["There is no need of yours."]

> *tuo adventu* nobis opus est *maturo*.   Cicero, *ad Att.* I.2.

5. **Manner**: expresses the manner of the action, usually with *cum* unless an adjective is used with the noun. Words like *modo, more, pacto, ratione, ritu, vi, via, iure* are ablatives of manner which have virtually become adverbs and are used without a preposition.

> rogo mane videas Plinium domi, sed plane mane, et *quoquo modo* efficias ne mihi irascatur.   Pliny I.5.

6. **The Ablative of Manner** may express **"in accordance with"** as in *sponte* (or *mea/sua sponte*) "of one's own accord" (i.e. voluntarily) or *mea sententia* "according to my way of thinking, in my opinion."

> Decessit Corellius Rufus et quidem *sponte* quod dolorem meum exulcerat.   Pliny I.12. ["Corellius Rufus has passed away, and in fact of his own will, which exacerbates my grief."]

7. **The Ablative of Accompaniment and Contention**: with *cum*

> quid tibi *cum mortuis meis*   Pliny I.5.

> cui non est *cum Cicerone* aemulatio   Pliny I.5.

> *mecum* tantum et *cum libellis* loquor   Pliny I.6.

8. **The Ablative of Degree of Difference** is used with comparatives and words implying comparison to indicate how great is the difference between the two things compared.

> *paulo* curatius   Pliny I.1.

> *multo* magis   Pliny I.9.

9. **Ablative of Description or Quality**: used with an adjective or genitive modifier.

> ad summam *animo forti* sitis   Cicero *ad Fam.* XIV.14.

> Villa usibus capax, non *sumptuosa tutela*.   Pliny II.27. ["The villa is large enough for convenience, and not of extravagant upkeep."]

10. **Ablative of Specification**: expresses the specific *respect* in which something is true or is done. [maior *natu*, "older"]

> Nam mala emptio semper ingrata, *eo* maxime, quod exprobare stultitiam domino videtur.   Pliny I.24. ["For a bad buy is always displeasing, in this respect especially: because it seems to accuse the buyer of stupidity."]

11. **Ablative Absolute**: expresses the time or circumstances of an action by means of a noun or pronoun [the subject of the construction] with a participle in agreement [the predicate] or a second noun or adjective in place of the participle. It is called "absolute" because it is grammatically independent of the rest of the sentence.

> Collegi *non servato temporis ordine* (neque enim historiam componebam), sed ut quaeque in manus venerat.   Pliny I.1.

> Mihi et temptandi aliquid et quiescendi *illo auctore* ratio constabit.   Pliny I.5.

> *L. Iulio Caesare, C. Marcio Figulo consulibus*   Cicero, *ad Att.* I.2.

C. Locative: IN

1. **Place Where**: usually with a preposition, with verbs of rest.

> Quin tu (tempus est enim) humiles et sordidas curas aliis mandas et ipse te *in alto isto pinguique secessu* studiis adseris?   Pliny I.3

In poetry and sometimes in prose, especially in later periods, the preposition may be omitted.

2. **Time When**: time when or within which is expressed by the ablative usually without a preposition (but sometimes with *in*).

> Haec *quo die* feceris necessaria ...   Pliny I.9.

> *Tertio et tricesimo anno* ut ipsum audiebam pedum dolore correptus est.   Pliny I.12. ["In his thirty-third year, so I used to hear him saying himself, he was attacked by gout."]

> *hoc tempore* Catilinam competitorem nostrum defendere cogitamus.   Cicero *ad Att.* 1.2.

Exercises

Translate:

A. Separation
1. Mauricius has not come [back] from exile.
2. Pliny is deprived of [lacks] his friend, a peach of a man [best man]
3. Regulus rejoiced in the prosecution [danger] of Rusticus.
4. Modestus was sent into Asia by the emperor.
5. Is fear stronger than love?

B-C. Instrumental, etc.

6. Pliny said that his mind was stimulated [excito (1)]by exercise [agitatio, -onis, f.]of the body.
7. Pliny uses and enjoys his own Laurentine estate [Laurentinum].
8. In my opinion it is not right to rely on the opinion of Regulus.
9. Does Pliny have need of our letters?
10. We are indeed trying to compete with Pliny.
11. No one is much more fearful than Regulus.
12. The son of Arria was of the highest courage.
13. Was Pliny older than Tacitus? [*older* = maior natu, see B.10, above]

B. Notes on Pronouns

RELATIVE, INTERROGATIVE, INDEFINITE (SEE A&G 147-152)

The **relative pronoun** is **qui, quae, quod** which can also be used as an adjective.

> iudices habemus *quos* voluimus   Cicero, *ad Att.* 1.2.

The relative pronoun or adjective very often begins a sentence in Latin to show the close connection with the previous thought. It is usually best to translate a relative pronoun at the beginning of a sentence as if it were a demonstrative.

> *quae* cum ita sint.   ["since these things are so"]
>
> *qua* re Ianuario mense, ut constituisti, cura ut Romae sis.   Cicero, *ad Att.* 1.2
>
> *quem* cum esse offensiorem arbitrarer   Cicero, *ad Att.* 1.5

The **interrogative pronoun** is **quis, quid**; the **interrogative adjective** is **qui, quae, quod** (declined like the relative)

> *quid* feci?   ["what have I done?"]
>
> *quod* facinus admisi?   ["what crime have I done?"]
>
> scin *quem* dicam?   Cicero, *ad Att.* 1.13

Other interrogative words

ecquis, ecquid	is there anyone who?
quisnam, quaenam, quidnam	who, pray? [Novi tibi *quidnam* scribam? Cicero, *ad Att.* 1.13.]
uter	which of two?
qualis	of what kind?
quantus	how great?
quantum	how much?
quotus	which in a series?

Indefinite pronouns and adjectives

aliquis, aliquid	someone, anyone
aliqui, aliqua, aliquod (adj.)	some, any [declined like *qui, quae, quod*; *aliqua* is used instead of *aliquae* except in the nom. pl. fem.] [Si te dolor *aliqui* corporis Cicero, *ad Fam.* 7.1.]
quis, quid	someone, anyone (after *si, nisi, num, ne*)
qui, qua, quod (adj.)	some, any
quispiam	someone, anyone

quisquam	anyone (at all) **quicquam** (neut.)
quidam	a certain [indicates a person not (necessarily) named, but known to the speaker: it is the most definite of the indefinite pronouns] [sed est miro *quodam* modo adfectus Cicero, *ad Att.* 1.5.]
quivis	anyone you will
quisque	each (one) [ut *quisque* in Epirum proficiscitur Cicero, *ad Att.* 1.13.]
uterque	each of two, both [*utrumque* laetor Cicero, *ad Fam.* 7.1.]
nonnulli	some few, more than one
nescio quis (prn), **nescio qui** (adj)	these are used as if they were single words and they play the part of indefinite pronouns, differing from *quidam* in that they are often contemptuous: Alcidamas **quidam** "one Alcidamas (whom I need not stop to describe further)" Alcidamas **nescio quis** "an obscure person called Alcidamas" [Mountford's Bradley's Arnold, 362]. The phrases *nescio quid, nescio quo modo, nescio quo pacto, quodam modo* are used to indicate something that is not easily defined or accounted for [Mountford's Bradley's Arnold, 363].
nescio quid	something (which I cannot define)
nescio quo modo	somehow or other
quicumque	whoever (indefinite relative)
quisquis	whoever (indefinite relative) both parts are declined, but only *quisquis, quidquid* (*quicquid*), *quoquo* are common (rare are *quemquem, quibusquibus*), see A&G 151b.
unusquisque	(gen. *uniuscuiusque*) every single one

EXERCISES

Identify the pronouns in these phrases from Pliny:

1.1 si quas paulo curatius scripsissem...
1.1 ut quaeque in manus venerat...
1.1 fiet ut eas quae adhuc neglectae iacent requiram...
1.3 quid agit?
1.3 ipse te ... adseris
1.3 effinge aliquid et exclude quod sit perpetuo tuum.
1.3 scio quem animum, quod horter ingenium.

1.5 vidistine quemquam M. Regulo timidiorem...

1.9 quod evenit mihi ...

3.5 a quo singulariter amatus hoc memoriae amici quasi debitum munus exsolvit.

3.5 si quid otii, iacebat in sole ...

3.5 Quid est enim quod non aut illae occupationes inpedire aut haec instantia non possit efficere?

3.5 Memini quendam ex amicis...

C. Review of Constructions using Verbs

SUBJUNCTIVE REVIEW 1: FORMS

The tenses of the subjunctive are the present, imperfect, perfect, and pluperfect. Only the present and imperfect show conjugational differences.

1. **Present:** "We seat all friars." In the present subjunctive, **E** is the characteristic vowel of the first conjugation **EA** of the second conjugation **A** of the third, and **IA** of the fourth and -i-stems of the third.

I	II	III	III-io	IV
		ACTIVE		
portem	teneam	ducam	capiam	sentiam
portes	teneas	ducas	capias	sentias
portet	teneat	ducat	capiat	sentiat
portemus	teneamus	ducamus	capiamus	sentiamus
portetis	teneatis	ducatis	capiatis	sentiatis
portent	teneant	ducant	capiant	sentiant
		PASSIVE		
porter	tenear	ducar	capiar	sentiar
porteris	tenearis	ducaris	capiaris	sentiaris
portere	teneare	ducare	capiare	sentiare
portetur	teneatur	ducatur	capiatur	sentiatur
portemur	teneamur	ducamur	capiamur	sentiamur
portemini	teneamini	ducamini	capiamini	sentiamini
portentur	teneantur	ducantur	capiantur	sentiantur

2. **Imperfect**: add personal endings to the present active infinitive.

I

Active: portarem, portares, portaret, portaremus, portaretis, portarent

Passive: portarer, portareris (portarere), portaretur, portaremur, portaremini, portarentur

II

Active: tenerem, teneres, teneret, teneremus, teneretis, tenerent

Passive: tenerer, tenereris (tenerere), teneretur, teneremur, teneremini, tenerentur

III and III-io

Active: ducerem, duceres, etc.

    caperem, caperes, etc.

Passive: ducerer, ducereris (ducerere) etc.

    caperer, capereris (caperere) etc.

IV

Active: sentirem, sentires, etc.

Passive: sentirer, sentireris (sentirere), etc.

3. **Perfect**

Active: add to the perfect stem the endings: -erim, -eris, -erit, -erimus, -eritis, -erint

    portaverim   tenuerim   duxerim   ceperim   senserim

Passive: use the perf. pass. participle and the present subjunctive of *sum* [sim, sis, sit, simus, sitis, sint; sometimes *fuerim, fueris*, etc. is used instead; in older Latin siem, etc.]

    portatus/-a sim   tentus/-a sim
    ductus/-a sim   captus/-a sim
    sensus/-a sim

[Be sure to make the participle agree in gender and number with the subject.]

4. **Pluperfect**

Active: add personal endings [-m, -s, -t, -mus, -tis, -nt] to the perfect active infinitive.

    portavissem   tenuissem   duxissem   cepissem   sensissem

Passive: use the perf. pass. participle and the imperfect subjunctive of *sum* [essem, esses, esset, essemus, essetis, essent; sometimes *fuissem* is used instead]

    portatus/-a essem   tentus/-a essem
    ductus/-a essem   captus/-a essem
    sensus/-a essem

Exercises

Form subjunctives of:

    scribo   publico, -are
    venio, -ire   iaceo, -are, -ui (active only)
    capio, -ere, capi, captum

Parse these subjunctive forms (numbers refer to letters in Pliny I):

scripsissem (1)	colligerem (1)	publicarem (1)
paeniteat (1)	requiram (1)	sit, sis (3)
reponatur (3)	horter (3)	velim (4)
facias (4)	irascerer (5)	recitaret (5)

Subjunctive Review 2:
Independent Uses of the Subjunctive

The numbers refer to letters of Pliny and Cicero. Fill in additional examples from your readings. Consult Allen and Greenough, 439-447.

    Volitive

        Hortatory "let us"
            "*Deflectamus*" inquam.   Pliny VI.20.

        Jussive "let him/her/it, let them"
            Hoc *sit* negotium tuum.   Pliny I.3.

    Prohibitive "don't"
            Cave nunciam oculos a meis oculis quoquam *demoveas* tuos...   Terence, *Adelphoe* 170. ["Do not take your eyes from my eyes..."].

    Prohibition is more commonly expressed by **noli** + infinitive; **ne** + subjunctive is also used.
            noli putare.   Cicero *ad Fam.* XIV.2.

    Deliberative "am I to"; "should I?"
            *patiamur*ne an *narremus* quoipiam?   Terence, *Adelphoe* 336. ["Are we to put up with it or should we tell it to someone?"]

    Optative "would that" "may ___!" often with **utinam** (sometimes with **ut**)
            Utinam illum diem *videam* cum tibi agam gratias quod me vivere coegisti!   Cicero *ad Att.* III.3.

Potential expresses a possibility: "would", "might"

> operti alioqui atque etiam *oblisi* pondere *essemus*.   Pliny VI.20.
> sed *velim* quam saepissime litteras mittatis.   Cicero *ad Fam.* XIV.2.

EXERCISES

Translate:
1. Are we to stay here at Misenum or flee?
2. Would that we see the day when our home is restored to us!
3. Let us return to Rome and wait for Tiro's recovery.
4. I would not wish you to go further away.
5. Let others take care of the humble concerns of your estate.

SUBJUNCTIVE REVIEW 3: SEQUENCE OF TENSES (A&G 482-5)

The tense of the subjunctive in a subordinate clause is governed by the rule of *sequence of tenses.*

If the main verb expresses present or future time, then the subjunctive is in the **present** or **perfect: primary sequence.**

If the main verb expresses past time (imperfect, pluperfect and usually perfect) then the **imperfect** or **pluperfect** subjunctive is used: **secondary** or **historical sequence.**

How to know which tense of the subjunctive to use:

In primary sequence, use the present subjunctive for an action going on *at the same time* as that of the main verb. *Nescio quid dicas.* "I do not know what you are saying."

In primary sequence, use the perfect subjunctive for an action that is *completed* at the time of the main verb. *Nescio quid dixeris.* "I do not know what you said/have said."

In secondary sequence, use the imperfect subjunctive for an action going on *at the same time* as the action of the main verb. *Nesciebam quid diceres.* "I was ignorant of what you were saying."

In secondary sequence, use the pluperfect subjunctive for an action that is *completed* at the time of the action of the main verb. *Nesciebam quid dixisses.* "I was ignorant of what you had said."

Although the perfect indicative is usually a secondary tense, sometimes primary sequence is used with it, especially in result clauses. The tense of the subjunctive to be used with a perfect indicative depends on the sense in which the perfect is used (as a simple past [secondary] or as a true perfect [primary], i.e. when translated by "have _____")

A subjunctive dependent directly on a perfect infinitive or a dependent perfect subjunctive requires secondary sequence, even if the main verb is primary.

A subjunctive dependent on an imperfect or pluperfect subjunctive uses secondary sequence.

In a purpose clause, the action of the verb cannot take place before that of the main verb and so only the present and imperfect subjunctives are used in purpose clauses.

To express future time in subjunctive clauses: in **primary** sequence, use the **present** subjunctive; in **secondary** sequence, use the **imperfect** subjunctive. For greater definiteness, the periphrastic forms -**urus sim**, -**urus essem** (the future active participle with the subjunctive of the verb *sum*) may be used. Temporal particles (such as *mox, brevi, statim*) may be used with the present or imperfect subjunctive to make futurity more clear.

SUBJUNCTIVE REVIEW 4:
USES IN SUBORDINATE CLAUSES (A&G 526-74)

The key to understanding the subjunctive is doubt or unreality.

1. **Purpose clauses** take present or imperfect subjunctive and are introduced by **ut** (uti), **ne, quo** (if there is a comparative in the main clause), or a relative pronoun or adverb.

> ut ne caeli quidem asperitas ullum studiis tempus
> *eriperet*   Pliny III.5.

Jussive noun clauses with **ut, ne** follow verbs like *moneo, rogo, oro, peto, postulo, precor, mando, impero, praecipio, persuadeo, hortor, permitto, concedo, non patior, volo* [ut is often omitted after volo].

> hortatus es ut epistulas ... *colligerem publicarem*que.   Pliny I.1.

> orabatque ut se ab iniuria oblivionis *adsereret*.   Pliny III.5

> cura ut Romae *sis*.   Cicero *ad Att.* 1.2.

> sed velim quam saepissime litteras *mittatis*.   Cicero *ad Fam.* XIV.2.

Verbs of hindering, preventing with **quin, quominus** [*prohibeo, impedio, deterreo*]

Purpose clauses can be introduced by relative pronouns.

quo magis *scires*   Pliny IV.13.

2. **Result clauses** are introduced by **ut, ut non** or a relative. A word like **tantus, talis, sic, ita, tam, adeo, tot**, forms of **is ea id**, often serves as a clue in the main clause.

tam diligenter libros avunculi mei lectitas ut habere omnes *velis* Pliny III.5.

dicere etiam solebat nullum esse librum tam malum ut non aliqua parte *prodesset*.   Pliny III.5.

Substantive clauses of result, after verbs like *facio, efficio*, and the impersonals, *fit, evenit, fieri potest, accedit, relinquitur*.

Superest ut nec te consilii nec me *paeniteat* obsequii.   Pliny I.1.

facies, si me diligis, ut quotidie *sit* Acastus in portu.   Cicero *ad Fam.* XVI.5.

3. **Relative clauses of characteristic** express a quality of a general or indefinite antecedent. They are often introduced by such expressions as **sunt qui, nemo est qui, quis est qui**, etc.

Effinge aliquid et exclude quod *sit* perpetuo tuum.   Pliny I.3.

Nec defuerunt qui fictis mentitisque terroribus vera pericula *augerent*.   Pliny VI.20.

si quid erit, quod te scire opus *sit* ...   Cicero *ad QF* II.10.

4. **Causal clauses** introduced by **cum** go into the subjunctive. Those introduced by **quod** and **quia** take the indicative unless they are giving a reason that is not the speaker's own, in which case they go into the subjunctive.

Coimus in porticu Liviae, cum alter ad alterum *tenderemus*. Pliny I.5.

5. **Temporal clauses** usually go into the indicative. But **cum** when it introduces a clause that gives the **general situation or circumstances** takes the subjunctive.

cum praefectus alae *militaret*   Pliny III.5.

6. Subordinate clauses in indirect statement take the indicative if they are true independently of the indirect quotation; otherwise they take the subjunctive.

> Scribis te absentia mea non mediocriter affici unumque habere solacium, quod pro me libellos meos *teneas*, saepe etiam in vestigio meo *colloces*. Pliny VI.7.

7. Indirect questions are introduced by verbs of asking, telling, wondering.

> quaerasque qui *sint* omnes...   Pliny III.5.

> Quantum dolorem *acceperim* et quanto fructu *sim privatus* et forensi et domestico Luci fratris nostri morte in primis pro nostra consuetudine tu existimare potes.   Cicero *ad Att.* I.5

> Vide, quanta **sit** in te suavitas.   Cicero *ad Fam.* XVI.5.

8. Concessive clauses: cum, quamvis, licet "although" take the subjunctive.

> Expalluit notabiliter, quamvis *palleat* semper. . .   Pliny I.5.

9. Proviso clauses with **dum, dummodo, modo** take the subjunctive.

> dummodo is tibi quidvis potius quam orationes meas *legerit* ... Cicero *ad Fam.* VII.1

10. Subjunctive with verbs of fearing "lest", "that"

> Verb of fearing with *ne* (lest, that) + subjunctive "I fear lest/that"
> Verb of fearing with *ut* (that not) or *ne non* (that not)

> Coepit vereri ne sibi *irascerer*. Pliny I.5.

> vereor ut Dolabella ipse satis nobis prodesse possit. Cicero, *ad Fam.* XIV.14

EXERCISES

Translate:
1. Pliny urged his friend to write something important.
2. See that you write something today.
3. Write something (of the sort) that everyone would want to read.
4. I am anxious since you have written me no letters for a long time.
5. I cannot understand why you have not written.
6. He is afraid that he is writing badly.

CONDITIONS (512-22)

Future less vivid: "should-would," present subjunctive in both clauses

> Nam si quem *interroges* "hodie quid egisti?", *respondeat*
> Pliny I.9.

Contrary to fact: in present time, imperfect subjunctive in both clauses [WERE... WOULD]; past time, pluperfect subjunctive in both clauses [HAD...WOULD HAVE]. They can also be in mixed time (one clause in present, the other in past) and they are not always complete "textbook" examples.

> Totum etiam *pollicerer,* nisi *timerem*   Pliny IV.13. [I would
> even promise the whole sum, if I were not afraid that...]
>
> si *respondissem* "bene"   Pliny I.5. [If I had answered "well"]
>
> surgebam, invicem, si *quiesceret,* excitaturus   Pliny VI.20.
> ["I was getting up, if she were sleeping [I was going] to
> awaken her"]
>
> si *comparer* illi, *sum* desidiosissimus.   Pliny III.5.
>
> *Scriberem* plura, si rem causamque *nossem.*   Cicero *ad Fam.*
> XII. 4.

Not all conditions take the subjunctive:

Future More Vivid Conditions: future or future perfect in both clauses.

English uses the present in the "IF" clause, but Latin uses the future or future perfect. "If you *do* this, you *will* do well": Si id *facies* bene *facies.*

> Si quas *addidero,* non *supprimam.*   Pliny I.1. ["If I add any I
> will not hold them back."]
>
> hoc numquam tuum *desinet* esse, si semel *coeperit.*   Pliny
> I.3.
>
> *respondebo* si de hoc centumviri *iudicaturi sunt.*   Pliny I.5.
>
> spero, si *absolutus erit,* coniunctiorem illum nobis *fore*
> in ratione petitionis; sin aliter *acciderit,* humaniter
> *feremus.*   Cicero *ad Att.* I.2.

Future Passive Periphrastic, Gerund, Gerundive (A&G 500-7)

1. **Gerundive with** *esse* "must be" "is to be" with **dative of agent** ("by"): Carthago *est delenda.*

   "dispicies ipse quid [*esse*] *renuntiandum* Regulo
   putes...   Pliny I.5.

2. **The gerund** is a verbal **noun, active** in meaning, **neuter singular**, in the oblique cases:

   -ndi -ndo -ndum -ndo

   non *auspicandi* causa sed *studendi* ...   Pliny III.5.

   abeundi consilium ...   Pliny VI.20.

3. **The gerundive** is a verbal **adjective, passive** in meaning, **all genders, numbers, and cases** in agreement with a noun or pronoun.

   intentione rei familiaris *obeundae* ...   Pliny I.3.

   quae te non tantum ad *legendos* eos verum etiam ad
   simile aliquid *elaborandum* possunt aemulationis stimulis
   excitare...   Pliny III.5.

   Multa ibi *miranda* ...   Pliny VI.20.

   ad eorum voluntatem mihi *conciliandam* maximo te mihi
   usui fore video.   Cicero *ad Att.* I.2.

Exercises

Translate:
1. If he adds any letters, he will publish them.
2. I would write more if I had anything to say.
3. Pliny's uncle wrote many books (worth) reading.
4. Pliny remained at his villa for the sake of writing.

D. Deponent Verbs

1. **Deponent verbs** are conjugated in the **passive** and do not have active[1] forms, but are translated as active or middle (reflexive).[2]

2. **Principal Parts**

    1 mor**or**, mor**ari**, mor**atus**/-a sum *delay*

    2 ver**eor**, ver**eri**, ver**itus**/-a sum *fear*

    3 lab**or**, lab**i**, lap**sa**/-us sum *slip, glide*

    3 io grad**ior** grad**i** gress**us**/a sum walk, step, go

    4 mol**ior**, mol**iri**, mol**itus**/-a sum *toil at*

3. **Deponents used in selected letters of Pliny:** [1] = 1st conjugation (like **moror**).

    * basic vocabulary words: should be learned

auguror [1] *prophecy*

auspicior [1] *take the auspices*

cunctor [1] *delay* **percunctor** *inquire* [Engl. *cunctation* = procrastination]

experior, -iri, expertus/a sum *try, test, put to the test* [> Engl. *experience, peril*; related to *empirical* < Greek]

* **fateor**, fateri, fassus/a sum *confess* [> Eng. *confess, professor, confiteor* = the confession] **confiteor** *confess* **profiteor** *offer*

* **fungor**, fungi, functus/-a sum *perform* [> Engl. *perfunctory, defunct*] **perfungor** *perform, undergo*

* **gradior**, -i, gressus/a sum *step, go* [> Engl. *ingredient, aggressive*] **aggredior** *approach, undertake*

* **hortor** [1] *urge, exhort* [> Engl. *hortatory, cohort*] **adhortor** *exhort*

labor, -i, lapsus/a sum *slip, glide, swoop* [> Engl. *lapse, elapse*] **dilabor** *glide away* **elabor** *glide out, slip away*

* **loquor**, loqui, locutus/-a sum *speak* [> Engl. *interlocutor, cirumlocution, loquacious*] **alloquor** *speak to address*

luctor [1] *struggle* [> Engl. *reluctant*] **eluctor** *struggle through*

miror [1] *marvel, wonder at* [> Engl. *miracle, mirage, mirror*] **admiror** *wonder at*

misereor, -'ri *feel pity* [> Engl. *commiserate*]

* **morior**, mori, mortuus/-a sum *die* [> Engl. *mortal*]

---

1 Except that they have participles of both voices: **sequens, secuturus** and **secutus, sequendus**. The perfect participle of deponents is usually active in sense, but sometimes passive. The future infinitive is always active in form.

2 The gerundive is passive in meaning and is found only in transitive verbs and intransitive verbs used impersonally. Most deponents are intransitive or middle.

moror [1] *delay, detain* < **mora** *delay* [> Engl. *moratorium*]
    commoror *linger*

* **nascor**, -i, nata/us sum *be born, arise, grow* [> Engl. *nascent, nature, naive*]

nitor, -i, nisus/nixus sum *lean upon, strive, rely*
    enitor *strive, struggle, make an effort, work one's way up*
    innitor *depend*

* **orior**, -iri, ortus/a sum *arise, spring* [> Engl. *orient, abortion*]

partior, -iri, partita/us sum *divide, share* [> Engl. *partition*]

* **patior**, pati, passa/us sum *suffer, bear, allow* [> Engl. *compatible, dispassionate*]

piscor [1] *fish* [< **piscis**, *fish*]

polliceor, -eri, pollicitus/a sum *promise*

precor [1] *pray* [> Engl. *deprecate, precarious*] **deprecor** *beg off, intercede*

proficiscor, -i, profecta/us sum *set out, depart*

recordor [1] *remember*

reminiscor, -i *call to mind, recollect, remember*

* **sequor**, -i, secuta/us sum *follow* [> Engl. *sequacious, executor*]
    exsequor *pursue, carry out* **prosequor** *accompany, present*
    subsequor *follow* **insector** [1] *attack*

SEMIDEPONENT **soleo**, -ere, solitus sum *be accustomed, be used to* [> Engl. *obsolescent*]

solor [1] *console, mitigate* **consolor** *comfort*

testor [1] *bear witness, give evidence* **detestor** *curse, deprecate*

tueor, -eri, tuta/-us *watch, guard, protect, defend, keep in mind* [> Engl. *tutelage*] **tutor** [1] *guard*

* **utor**, uti, usa/us sum *use* (+ ABL.) [> Engl. *abuse, utile*]

vagor [1] *wander* [> Engl. *vagabond*] **pervagor** *rove over*

venor [1] *hunt*

vereor -eri, verita/us sum *fear* **revereor** *feel awe*

versor [1] *engage in, practice, be in* **adversor** *resist* **obversor** *hover before, appear*

vescor *feed on*

See A&G 190-192 for the conjugation of deponents and for a list of irregular deponents and semideponents.

COMPOUND VERBS USING PREFIXES

Linguistic principles for compounding:

1. **Vowel weakening**: after a prefix **a** > **i** or **e**: capere > incipere; captum > praeceptum; and **e** > **i** tenere > continere.

   When a prefix is added:

   a or **e** > **i** before a single consonant: facere > deficere; specere > conspicere.

   a > **e** before two or more consonants: factum > defectum.

2. **Assimilation**: [base, simil-, *like*] the act of making one thing like [*to* = ad-] another. Sometimes a consonant at the end of a prefix changes so that it will be easier to pronounce before the first consonant of the base.

   For example:

   ad-, *to* becomes ac- before c̲; as- before s̲

   ad-cedo > accedo ad-sumo > assumo

   com-, *with, together* becomes cor- before r

   com-ripio > corripio

   After **ex**-, *out* an initial s̲ is dropped in English, but retained in Latin.

   ex-spectare > Engl. expect

List of Latin prefixes with special reference to compound verbs in Seneca. Asterisks mark the most productive prefixes. The variations are listed with the prefixes.

1. **a-, ab-, abs-* *away from, off, badly* [The usual form is ab-; a- is used before m, p, v; abs before c, t.]

   Examples: abruptus (*broken off*); avertere (*turn away*); abstractus (drawn away); aufero [Sen. 1]

2. **ad-* *to, toward, against, intensely* [ad- appears also as ac- (before c, q), af-, ag-, al-, an-, ap-, ar-, as-, at-, and a- (before sc, sp, st, gn).]

   Examples: adventus (*a coming towards*); accuratus (*attended to*); annotare (*add notes to*); assentire (*feel to, agree*); accipio [Sen. 1]; attendere [Sen. 1]; agnosco [Sen. 31]

3. **ambi-** *around, about, on both sides* [amb- before vowels]

Examples: ambiguus (*going around, uncertain*) [cf. Eng. ambidextrous, *right-handed on both sides*]; ambitio (*going around, canvassing for votes*)

4. ***ante-*** *before, in front of, ahead of*

Example: antecedere (*go before*)

5. ***circum-*** *around*

Examples: circumflectere (*wheel around*); circumspicere (*look around*)

6. **cis-** *on this side of, on the near side of*

Examples: Cisalpinus (*on this side of the Alps*); cismontanus *dwelling on the near side of the mountains* [cf. Engl. cislunar *on this side of the moon*

7. ***com-*** *with, together* [com- before b, p, m; cor- before r; col- before l; co-before h, gn and usually before vowels; con- before all other consonants.]

Examples: colloquium (*a speaking together*); corrodere (*gnaw thoroughly, nibble away*); cogere < co + agere (*drive together, compel*); complector [Sen. 1]; congero [Sen. 31]

8. ***de-*** *down from, off, utterly;* this prefix may imply removal or cessation and it may give a bad (or negative) sense to the word.

Examples: devolvere (*roll down*); deformis (*ill/badly formed*); demens (*out of one's mind, mad*); desero [Sen. 31]

9. ***dis-*** *apart, in different directions, at intervals;* it can also have a negative force. [di- before voiced consonants; dif- before f; in English derivatives, sometimes de- under French influence: depart, defy]

Examples: differre (*bear/carry apart*); dispellere (*push in different directions*); differo [Sen. 1]

10. ***ex-, e-*** *out from, out of, off, away, away from, thoroughly* [ef before f]

Examples: eventum (*outcome*); extollere (*raise out*); exspectare (*look out, await*); effluo [Sen. 1]; elabor [Sen. 1]; eripio [Sen. 1]; evenio [Sen. 1]; excido (cado) [Sen. 1]; eligo [Sen. 31]

11. **extra-** [variant, extro-] *outside, beyond*

Example: extraordinarius (*beyond the rank*)

12. ***in-*(1)** *in, into, on, toward, against* [il- before l; im- before b, m, p; ir- before r; in English derivatives, sometimes en- under French influence.]

Examples: incidere (*cut into*); impellere (*push on*); imputor [Sen. 1]; incipio [Sen. 1]; inicio [Sen. 1]; impendo [Sen. 31]; incubo [Sen. 31]

13. ***in-*(2)** *not, lacking, without* [i- before gn; other changes as in-(1)]

Examples: illepidus (*inelegant, churlish*); ignobilis (*not noble, unknown, low-born*); inermis [< in + arma] (*unarmed*); ignosco (*forgive*) [Sen. 1]

14. ***inter-*** *among, between, at intervals, mutually, each other* [intel- before l]

Examples: intercipere (*take between, embezzle, steal*); intercedere (*come between*); intellectus (*choosing between, understanding*); interrogo [Sen. 1]

15. **infra-** (Rare) *below, beneath, inferior to, after, later*

   Example: infraforanus (*under the Forum*)

16. **intra-** (Rare) *in, within, inside of*

   Example: intraclusus (*shut in, enclosed*)

17. **intro-** *in, into, inward*

   Example: introducere (*lead into*)

18. *ob- *toward, against, across, in the way of, opposite to, down, for, out of, intensely* [o- before m; oc- before c; of- before f; op- before p.]

   Examples: oblongus (*long across*); offerre (*bring for*); obduratus (*hardened against*); obdo [Sen. 31]

19. *per- *through, by, thoroughly, away, badly, to the bad* [pel- before l]

   Examples: permeare (*pass through*); perfidia (*bad faith*); pellucidus (*thoroughly clear/bright*); perdo [Sen. 1]

20. *post- *behind, after*

   Examples: postponere (*put after*); postmeridianus (*in the afternoon*)

21. *prae- [Engl. pre-] *before, in advance, in front of, headfirst, at the end*

   Examples: praecedere (*go before*); praetendere (*spread in front, give as an excuse*); praecipio (*give instructions*) [Sen. 1]

22. **praeter-** [Engl. preter-] *past, beyond*

   Examples: praeteritus (gone past) praetermissio (omission, passing over)

     praetereo (eo ire) [Sen. 1]   praeterveho [Sen. 31]

23. *pro- *forth, for, forward, publicly, instead o* [before vowels, prod-]

   Examples: proclamare (*shout publicly/forth*); procedere (*go forward*); prospicio [Sen. 1]

24. *re- *back, again, against, behind* [red- before vowels]

   Examples: repello (*push back*); recordari (*bring back to mind*); redimere < emere (*buy back*); reddo (*give back, render an account of*) [Sen. 1]; redigo (ago) [Sen. 1]; remaneo [Sen. 1]

25. *se- *aside, apart, away* [sed- before vowels]

   Examples: securus (*away from/free from care*); seducere (*lead apart*)

26. *sub- *under, inferior, secondary, less than, in place of, secretly* [suc- before c; suf- before f; sug- before g; sum- before m; sup- before p; sur- before r; sometimes sus- before c, p, t.]

   Example: subtrahere (*draw from under*); subduco [Sen. 1]; subripio [Sen. 1]; succurro (*aid, help*) [Sen. 1]

27. **subter-** *beneath, secretly*

   Example: subterfugere (*evade, flee in secret*)

28. ***super-** over, above, excessively, beyond* [In English derivatives, sometimes sur- under French influence: surtax, surrealism, surcharge]

   Example: superimponere (*put over/on top*); supersum [Sen. 1]

29. ***trans-** across, over, beyond, through, very* [tra-, tran-]

   Examples: transportare (*carry across/over*); transgredi (*step across*); transcurro [Sen. I.1]

SUGGESTIONS FOR
FURTHER READING

An asterisk indicates a work recommended for both secondary and college students.

General

* Hammond, N. G. L. and H.H.Scullard (edd.). *The Oxford Classical Dictionary*, 2nd ed. Oxford: Clarendon Press, 1978.
* Kenney, E.J. and W. V. Clausen (edd.). *The Cambridge History of Classical Literature, Vol. II: Latin Literature*, Cambridge: Cambridge University Press, 1982.

Everyday Life, Letters

Hooper, Finley and Matthew Schwartz, *Roman Letters: History from a Personal Point of View*. Detroit: Wayne State University Press, 1991.
* Kenyon, Frederic G. *Books and Readers in Ancient Greece and Rome*, 2nd ed.. Oxford: Clarendon Press, 1951.
Nicholson, John. "The Delivery and Confidentiality of Cicero's Letters." *CJ* 90 (1994):33-63.
*Shelton, Jo-Ann. *As The Romans Did: A Sourcebook in Roman Social History*. New York: Oxford University Press, 1998, 2nd ed.

Cicero

* Shackleton Bailey, D.R. *Cicero, Epistulae ad familiares*. Cambridge: Cambridge University Press, 1977.
_____ *Cicero, Letters to Atticus*. Cambridge: Cambridge University Press, 1965-70.
Classen, Jo-Marie. "Documents of a Crumbling Marriage: The Case of Cicero and Terentis." *Phoenix* 50 (1996):208-232.
Tyrrell, Robert Yelverton. *Cicero in his letters*. London, Macmillan; New York, St. Martin's Press, 1962.

Pliny

Birley, Anthony R. *Onomasticon to the Younger Pliny*: Letters *and* Panegyric. München/Leipzig: K. G. Saur, 2000.

Hoffer, Stanley E. *The Anxieties of Pliny the Younger*. Atlanta: Scholars Press, 1999.

* Sherwin-White, A. N. *The Letters of Pliny: a historical and social commentary*. Oxford, Clarendon Press, 1966.

Seneca

Summers, Walter C. *Seneca, Select Letters*. London: Macmillan, 1910 (repr. 1962). For Seneca's "pointed" style.